GREAT GROUPING STRATEGIES

Ways to Formally and Informally Group Students to Maximize Their Social, Emotional, and Academic Learning

By
Ronit M. Wrubel

SCHOLASTIC
PROFESSIONAL BOOKS

NEW YORK • TORONTO • LONDON • AUCKLAND • SYDNEY
MEXICO CITY • NEW DELHI • HONG KONG • BUENOS AIRES

Acknowledgments

I give my eternal gratitude to all of the extraordinary children who have helped me to learn, live, and love by sharing their hearts and minds with me.

I give my fervent thanks to all of the families, teachers, administrators, and staff members that I have had the pleasure of working with over all of these years, and to my forever home, P.S. 3. My thanks also to Jodi Weisbart for her encouragement during this venture. An extra special thank you to Lois Blank, Lucy Rubin, Dan Zulawski, John Melser, Natalie Dean, Cindy Wang, and my always co-teacher, Kristen GoldMansour, for giving me the right start and for being with me all along.

My first effort at writing a professional book came along beautifully because of the dedication, wisdom, and knowledge of Merryl Meleska Wilbur. I thank you times a million! I give my tremendous respect and endless appreciation to Joanna Davis-Swing, Wendy Murray, and Terry Cooper, for the honor of letting me share my teaching with others, and for brilliantly guiding me through every step of this process; to Shelley Harwayne for being an inspiration and wonderful mentor; and to Hindy List, whose intelligence about teaching and learning, whose devotion to educating children, and whose constant support of my work made this book possible.

And to my family and friends, who wholeheartedly championed me,
(and put up with me), throughout this amazing endeavor...Thank you.
I love you always and all ways!

Teachers may photocopy the designated reproducible pages for classroom use. No other part of this publication may be reproduced in whole or in part, or stored in a retrieval system, or transmitted in any form or by any means, electronic, mechanical, photocopying, recording, or otherwise, without written permission of the publisher. For information regarding permission write to Scholastic Inc., 555 Broadway, New York, NY 10012.

Cover design by James Sarfati
Cover and interior photographs on pages 9, 20, 45, 65, 81, and 94 by Nina Roberts.
All other photos courtesy of author.
Interior design by Solutions by Design, Inc.

ISBN: 0-439-30467-9

Copyright © 2002 by Ronit M. Wrubel
All rights reserved. Printed in the U.S.A.

2 3 4 5 6 7 8 9 10   40   08 07 06 05 04 03

TABLE OF CONTENTS

Dedicated to Dad, Mom, Helen, Beni, Alex, Harry, and Karen,
for allowing me the privilege of being a member of the best group that there is
in this universe: my family. You are the wind beneath my wings!

FOREWORD

Gone are the Bluebirds and Robins. Gone are the carved-in-stone student groupings based on children's standardized test scores. Gone are the laminated lists of group members, decided in September and lasting through June. Instead, Roe Wrubel, a teacher's teacher, opens up her heart and mind and lets us look inside, helping educators understand how she goes about creating wise and wonderful working groups, ones in which children appreciate one another and graciously learn to teach and learn alongside one another.

It's no surprise that parents always take comfort in placing their children in Roe Wrubel's confident and capable hands. She makes it look so easy to exquisitely take care of students' social, emotional, and academic needs. Each time I visit Roe's classroom, I leave in awe, filled with such questions as, "How does she do it? How does she get such young children to be on task every minute? How does she create such seamless teaching moments? How does she cover so much curriculum in any one school day? How does she keep her classroom so orderly and beautiful?" With the publication of this book, I now have the answers to my many questions.

Through practical suggestions written in easy-to-read prose, the author helps us to understand how she capitalizes on what she knows about each of her students to create a model early-childhood classroom. Roe is able to maximize her teaching time and simultaneously create a joyously child-centered classroom because she is thoughtful and deliberate in planning for instruction. And at the heart of all her instruction is her steadfast belief in the power of small circles. Roe highly values the importance of having just the right small circle of students working with her and with one another, at just the right time.

As the superintendent of Roe's school district, I am particularly delighted that she has chosen to publish the story of her classroom. I often suggest to our beginning teachers that they visit Roe's calm, energizing, and rigorous classroom. Of course, any one visit is never enough. Now, through the reading of this book, teachers can establish long-term mentor relationships with the author as they dig into each chapter and listen as Roe reveals why she makes the decisions she does, how she turns those decisions into effective classroom interactions, and how she continuously reflects on her practice in order to make every minute count for each and every student in her diverse New York City classroom.

Readers should consider this book as their very own visit to Roe Wrubel's classroom, and the reading, rereading, and highlighting of the strategies on each and every page as an opportunity to hang out with Roe in the staff room, chatting with her about her practice and listening to her behind-the-scenes explanation of what makes her classroom hum.

On September 11, 2001, Roe Wrubel was one of those heroic New York City teachers who marched her children to safety as they fled their school building just three blocks from ground zero. I am eternally grateful to her for her wisdom and bravery that day, but it is her everyday brilliance and risk-taking that defines her role as an exemplary educator. Each and every day, through her teaching and her writing, Roe Wrubel inspires us to refine our practice and reminds us to take pride in being part of such a scholarly profession.

— Shelley Harwayne, Superintendent, Community School District 2
Senior Superintendent, Manhattan, New York City Public Schools

Introduction

"What a child can do in cooperation today, he can do alone tomorrow."
—Lev Vygotsky

When I think about my own elementary-school experiences, I still remember the feeling I had every time I averted my eyes from my own work. I felt as if I was cheating, defrauding myself and my teacher by looking around at what other students were doing. I went to school in an atmosphere of isolation: separate desks, separate worksheets and workbooks, no creativity, no interaction, and no talking to each other—*ever*. And while we were told to share our "things," we were not encouraged to share our learning. I got the picture that what was valued in school was disconnection from the real world and from the other children. We listened and learned from the teacher, the ever-present figure in the front of the room. We gave forth the information that we took in from that one source, and were told our worth by a red number on the top of a piece of paper. In the end, I did advance, I did learn, and I did just fine—on my own, by myself, just me.

It wasn't until college, in my education courses, that I actually began to work with other students on a regular basis. I began to see the value in sharing ideas, sharing knowledge, and sharing frustrations, and these newfound experiences gave me an opportunity to rethink what I knew about children and about teaching and learning. How do children learn and how do they learn best? How important is it to engage in conversations and activities with others? What academic and social benefits are heightened because of group experiences? What level of pleasure is provided by working together? When is it advantageous for children to work alone?

I took these questions with me into my student teaching and eventually into my own classroom teaching experiences. I have devoted much of my planning time to thinking of ways of grouping students to allow them to work and discover things together with the goal of increasing knowledge and learning to value interdependence. Over the years, I have arranged my students *strategically* in countless ways, formally and informally and in all subject areas, to maximize growth and learning. Some efforts worked better than others. What I have found, overwhelmingly so, is that children do learn better when they share learning together. Surely this concept is no longer entirely new to most teachers; I haven't invented the wheel here. But from my own classroom experiences, and now through undertaking this book to illustrate strategic grouping and its many benefits, I have reached some philosophical and practical conclusions: Given the chance to learn from and with each other, children excel—socially, emotionally, and academically. And there are, indeed, specific strategies for grouping that are both effective and manageable for you and your students. I will share them with you here.

CHAPTER ONE

MIX AND MATCH

Grouping Students in Different Ways

During my first year of teaching, I had a class full of active, bright children (and happily, that continues to be the case every year). I quickly realized that my students had a lot to say, a lot to ask, and a lot of energy to spare. And I recognized as well that I couldn't—and didn't want to—have them working as a whole group all of the time; that I couldn't possibly spend as much time as I would like with each child individually; and that I didn't want to limit my students' interactions. So in order to meet my instructional goals, I began pairing students up or assembling them into groups, inviting them to work together. I noticed immediately that children were working well together, learning cooperatively, and having fun in the process. And after a while, I also began to notice how varying the groups strategically could be instrumental in maximizing that effect. I became fully committed to providing students with plenty of opportunities to work and learn from each other, and strategic grouping became an integral part of my planning and teaching.

Don't get me wrong; I don't think that every class activity should be done in groups. Children need to work independently, and some prefer to do so. Certain partnerships or groups—no matter how well intentioned—are not successful. What I do know is that flexibility in arranging and using groups has made my teaching and my students' learning much more effective—and enjoyable.

While watching children over the years, I have seen the numerous, wonderful benefits that arise from a variety of group work. Many students have been propelled forward academically because they had the chance to talk with and learn from another child who was an expert in a subject they were struggling with. For some, grouping created an opportunity to enhance their school experiences by solidifying friendships based on the amount of time students were able to spend with each other. For others, group learning allowed them to discover new, interesting, and admirable qualities in each other when they were able to work closely with children who they might not otherwise have gotten to know very well. This environment provided students with welcoming, fun-filled days—a positive learning experience, to be sure.

Prominently posted on the main bulletin board in my classroom is this message:

WHY?
Always Ask and Try to Answer Questions

My students know that **"WHY"** is my favorite word in the English language. I love this word because of the possibilities it opens up. Why allows us to question our world, to question ourselves, and to seek the kind of knowledge that keeps us learning and growing throughout time. All children have a natural curiosity, a quest for knowledge, a drive for understanding. I don't believe that every question has an answer, but I do believe that there is much to be gained in the exploration. And in life, the best explorations are usually collaborative ones.

One of the roles that I see for myself as a teacher is to help children pursue investigations. As a mentor and guide, I try to orchestrate the experiences of my students toward inquiring about the world we live in. I want to help them to know who they are and where they are. School is about so much more than reading, writing, and arithmetic. Adults spend much of their time interacting with others, making decisions together, and sharing information. We are in a profession that grants us the fortune to help children learn how to do these things effectively to achieve their goals and to explore the world. But to do this, they need basic learning skills and strategies. They need the opportunities to work in different subject areas and on different problems. They also need to learn *together*.

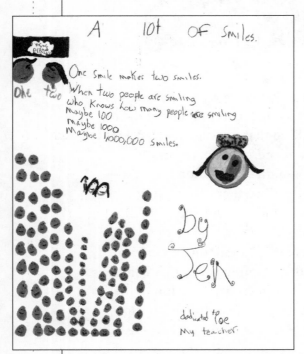

Students experience the joy and rewards of working together.

The Benefits of Varied Grouping

The benefits of varied grouping are manifold, and I discover more every year. One of the main goals of teaching is to help children achieve both independence and interdependence. As I ponder my experiences each year, I see how allowing children to work together has helped them move away from egocentricity and toward autonomy. The following is just a sampling of the positive effects of grouping that I've observed.

Conversation is a two-way process. Being able to *get a point across* is a learned skill, one that is better learned in the context of real work. In my classes, the ability to articulate ideas is practiced and developed through group work because students must find ways of talking so that the other group members understand what they are trying to say. By having children spend a good deal of time talking to each other about specific topics, they get to practice their verbal skills. *Taking in new information* is also something that increases with experience. As children work on listening to each other, they learn how to ask clarifying questions, to respond to the thinking of others, and to find ways to compromise on task outcomes.

Partnership and group formats (both large and small) help ensure that all students get to know each other, creating a cohesive class community. By spending time with each other in different ways, the children learn more about who their classmates are personally and who they are in the realm of the classroom. As they become more aware of the interesting things that they can all say and do, students become a kind of family. Eventually, they find ways in which they can help each other and learn from each other—and will even choose to spend time with kids that they might not have been immediately drawn to.

Groups can positively focus attention on students' talents and skills. Indeed, children have many strengths, socially and academically, but those strengths are sometimes hidden by behavioral or academic struggles. Rather than focusing only on the weaknesses and needs of others (the way traditional instructional formats often do), strategically-formed groups give students the chance to see the things that other children are capable of. Groups can be flexibly arranged so that struggling students are placed in a situation in which they can exhibit their strengths. It is extremely beneficial to learning and to friendships when students see others as their equals—and see themselves as contributing members of a class community. Peer efforts, experiences, and progress can foster achievement for the entire class.

Another huge benefit of having children work together is that, as they get ideas from each other, *they begin to stretch their own thinking and skills.* While I work very diligently to create a non-competitive environment, I also want students to broaden their knowledge base and performance skills. When students share what they do, when they get to see what other children are planning and accomplishing, they will be encouraged to try these things on their own. Conversely, when students work in isolation, their progress is solely determined by what they are doing themselves. When they work with others, they have the occasion to see and discuss new strategies and topics. Instead of remaining in a holding pattern with what they can do, students can try out new things and move forward at a quicker pace.

There are countless benefits to working in groups. Although no list of rewards can be complete, I feel it is important to highlight some of the principal benefits.

Participating in a variety of groups helps students:

✤ Develop communication and interpersonal skills

✤ Learn about, understand, accept, and appreciate differences among peers

- ✪ Become an integral part of a community
- ✪ Solidify their academic knowledge and skills by modeling for and working with their peers
- ✪ Get to know all of their classmates and develop relationships with peers outside their circle of friends
- ✪ Learn from each other and regard peers as valid resources
- ✪ Think through and talk about new ideas with others
- ✪ Challenge themselves and each other
- ✪ Enjoy learning!

During my years of teaching, I have noticed that having children work with each other has actually enabled the advances in the education I intended for my students. Group work has also facilitated several unintentional advances.

The following conversations illustrate the kinds of learning that can take place during group work—all without teacher intervention.

Group Work in Action

TWO STUDENTS SOLVE THEIR OWN PROBLEM

It was partner reading time and I was having a conference with two children while a child from another nearby partnership approached me.

Debby: *Roe, Luca and I can't agree on which book to read next!*

Roe: *I'm in the middle of a conference; try to talk it out again, and I'll be with you soon.*

(This is what I heard next:)

Debby: *Luca, Roe's busy, and I want to start reading.*

Luca: *But I don't want to read another* Bailey School Kids *book. We've read two of them already.*

Debby: *And I don't want to read* The Time Warp Trio.

Luca: *But you chose the last book we read. Oh, well, why don't we put these books in our independent book baskets and try to think of a new book that we can do for partner reading?*

Debby: *Do you remember when we heard* The Stories Julian Tells *for read aloud?*

Luca: *That was great! I loved Huey. I know there are more books in that series.*

Debby: *Bingo! Let's go check it out.*

TEACHER'S TAKE: When I got back to Debby and Luca, I pretended that I hadn't heard what happened and asked them to tell me how they decided on reading *More Stories Julian Tells*. The students told me they decided to choose a different book, one that they could both agree on. What Debby and Luca figured out on their own was even better than what I would have initially suggested. My first thought was to tell Debby and Luca to take turns reading the books that they both wanted to read. There might have been some reluctance from one or both of the children as they read those two books. Instead, they found a book they were both excited about, and they reminded me of another idea for what to suggest when students are trying to choose a new book to read together.

STUDENTS LEARN TO HELP ME AND EACH OTHER

When I don't want to interrupt a child I'm listening to, I hold up my forefinger as another child approaches; this is my signal to wait a minute. Sometimes the kids go back to what they were doing and sometimes they stand and wait. Sasha was usually a child who waited—and kept calling my name while waiting.

Sasha: *Roe, Roe, I don't know how to use the scale.*

I held up my finger, since I was talking to Mikael.

Sasha: *Roe, are you done yet?*

I held up my finger again and whispered to her that I would be done soon. Sasha continued to stand there. Then, another group member called to her.

Krista: *Sasha, you're in my group.*

Sasha: *But I don't know what to do.*

Krista: *But you have to give it a try.*

Sasha: *I'm waiting for Roe.*

Krista: *I've used these scales during explore time. I'll help you out if you come back. Jesse got the wrong blocks, so I need you to help me get the other blocks anyway.*

TEACHER'S TAKE: Krista was not only paying attention to whom she was working with, but she was also noticing that I was busy. In helping out Sasha, she was helping me, too.

While I don't like to make children wait for me (especially when they need assistance), I know that the only way I can have productive conferences with all my students is to give the proper time and attention to them when it is their turn. By giving my students the tools to know how to work with each other, I am also giving myself the gift of being able to focus on my current meeting. I have learned so much from watching and listening to my students as they work with each other.

Use Grouping Strategies to Support Instruction

Determine Long-Term Goals

When I think about all of the different subject areas that I will cover in any given school day, month, or year, my first step is to focus on the big idea. I need to decide what my long-term goal is for a particular subject. Then I can start to delineate the lessons that will help bring the children towards that goal and to consider how to incorporate groups most effectively. I must also think about which grouping strategies will work best. I ask myself the following questions to clarify my purpose:

1. **What is the objective I have for my students?**

If I would like the children to learn that an adjective is a word that describes a noun, I may have them work in a reading partnership to look for examples in a copy of a text. Each partner would take turns underlining adjectives, then circling nouns. They would talk about what they were noticing as they worked and later share their findings with the class.

2. What concepts are they ready to learn?

When I want students to understand the concept of how an environment affects the way animals live, I set up learning center groups and then have each group study an animal. The heterogeneously grouped children provide each other with their own background knowledge of the animal and its environment. Next, they do research on their animal, share new information, and later report their findings to the class. Each group should describe the animal they studied and what they learned about its habits, which are often affected by surroundings.

3. What skills do the students need to practice/develop?

As children need to develop measurement skills, I may have them form a "Thank You Very Much" partnership so that they can measure certain items in the classroom together. When students help each other with measuring tasks, they get to practice being precise and can take turns holding measuring tools and recording results. They also learn some of the benefits of teamwork—how collaborating can make a task easier and more enjoyable.

4. What topics are interrelated and cross-curricular?

During a nonfiction literature genre study, my goals of having the children research the properties of a particular genre, write about that genre, and expand their understanding of book genres in general would be aided by setting up an interest-based group of about five children. With common interests as a bond, the children would more readily get into the work necessary to use the genre study as a way of linking reading and writing.

5. What modes and roles will I plan for in the lessons?

When I think about the kind of activity I plan for a lesson, I need to figure out which children I want to become the models for others who may have trouble, or which students need to be in the position of being the expert. I could plan a math lesson that involves three children—one writing out a problem, one figuring out the answer, and one drawing figures to match the mathematical equation. A child who is still learning how to figure out those kinds of problems would still be an integral part of the group (writing down the problem or drawing figures), and a child uncomfortable with drawing would not have to take on that role. Afterwards, one or all of the students would explain their problem and the results to the entire class. Not only would the child who solved the problem benefit from being the "expert," but those drawing figures, writing down the problem, and sharing with the class would feel important as well. Best of all, the students will see that they each have skills that contributed to completing the assignment.

6. How can I support students as they complete the assignment(s)?

Because class time can be so limited, I know that I can only help one or two pairs of children per session who are peer editing a writing project. So when I set up peer editing groups, I make sure that one of the students is more proficient at spelling and punctuation, so that all of the groups can be engaged in real work, even if I am not with them. The grouping decisions I make provide support for all the students as I hold my conferences with one team at a time.

7. How can the class share in the information learned?

As I watch students work during an assignment, I make notes about which groups have used the strategies that I want to highlight. When we have a "share" meeting at the end of the lesson, I call upon those children to explain what they have done and how they went about it. For example, during an exercise comparing characters from two different stories, I might ask the children who understood and talked about their characters' emotions to describe those emotions to the whole class. I would then ask children who were observing to tell what they heard in their own words, thus holding them accountable for listening to and thinking about the information others were giving them.

8. How can I assess the activity's effectiveness?

Looking back on what the children have done allows me to know if my planning goals have been met, and if the students I targeted for incidental experiences—academic or social—received what I planned for. For instance, when I listen to a group of children talk about what each child did to build a model of the solar system, I will know if my plan to have a quiet student be involved in the decision-making process actually worked.

These kinds of questions are critical to good instruction. And giving students the chance to work together in diverse groups is also essential. By mixing and matching the children, formally and informally, you will be able to address the many needs and interests of your students. Structuring appropriate groups and partnerships that fit the subject, goal, and lesson is really the best way you can help children acquire information and reach their potential.

Make Grouping Decisions That Enhance Instructional Decisions

As I plan lessons, I think about what groupings would help my students meet the learning goals I have set. I may want students to practice book talks, solve a math problem, or edit their papers, and I need to determine what grouping would help students best achieve these goals. I may decide to have children give book talks in groups of four, so they hear several examples and get plenty of feedback. And often, for solving math problems, I may choose to form groups of three, since everyone could participate in such a small group. Working with partners on peer editing would allow students to focus on just one paper at a time. In the next chapter, I'll discuss the many grouping possibilities that I have used and developed over the years. It may be impossible (and impractical given the make-up of your class) to utilize all of the formats I've devised, but I've found that having such a large repertoire under my belt makes my planning and implementation go more smoothly. As I reflect on and try out various group strategies, I determine which ones will work for a given set of students in a particular year.

What never ceases to amaze me is that when I listen in on a group or assess the outcome of a group activity, I inevitably find that many other things—besides my stated goal—have transpired, and these "side effects" are often just as valuable as the academic objective. A good example is the partner reading between Debby and Luca that I mentioned earlier. I have the children read with partners so that they can support each other as they decode and try to comprehend a given text. But as the conversation between Debby and Luca showed, they were able to move beyond my goals for them. The partners successfully negotiated the choice of a book. After expressing opinions, they were able to make a mutually satisfying choice. In this case, partner reading also resulted in an opportunity to use and develop social skills.

Additionally, I recognized that their shared enthusiasm for the book would be a strong factor for keeping them engaged in the text. That motivation served to aid and enhance what I

Group work creates friendships as students grow together emotionally, socially, and academically.

had initially planned for their reading experience. In giving children math problem-solving activities in small groups, my main purpose is to have them help each other complete the task. But as we saw, Sasha was feeling lost in her group; she needed to learn how to use the scales before she could help solve the problem. Krista was able to help refine Sasha's understanding of the materials. So, when I got to sit with that group, I was able to focus them all on the actual assignment (rather than give a mini-lesson on using scales). Remember, nothing is learned in a vacuum, and no learning experience can be confined to one, finite outcome. Group work is a great way to provide a multi-faceted learning experience for your students.

Use Grouping Strategies to Support Students' Social and Emotional Growth

COMMUNITY (noun): *a place where children and adults live and learn together.*

School is a social institution. Students and teachers come together every day bringing a whole range of experiences, desires, and problems. The classroom, the space inhabited together for a good part of each week, therefore needs to be a place where everyone can learn—not only academic subjects, but also how to get along as a community of individuals. Thus, it is essential to consider both the class as a whole and the "whole student" when planning for the year.

Children must be allowed to express themselves. They must learn how to talk to each other, play with each other, negotiate their way through difficult situations, explore with each other and, of course, learn together. There is no better way to help students do this than to empower them by modeling appropriate behavior and providing plenty of opportunities for them to practice in varied group experiences. (Chapter Five discusses modeling and offers a number of specific examples.)

In addition to modeling, it's essential to observe students' behavior and needs closely and respond accordingly. Teachers can help students improve their discourse skills by portraying positive interactions and by interceding as necessary when they are trying out discussions or lessons on their own that might be difficult. Initially, like me, you'll probably spend a good deal of time encouraging quieter students to become a part of the gathering, and helping very verbal kids learn to listen to others. It's also important to facilitate work and play for children who tend to go on their own. Set up experiences that require teamwork, value and praise good collaboration, and encourage families to follow up and help develop these relationships with phone calls and play dates when possible. In my class, I always make it a point to tell the children when I learn something from how they are working together, and I commend the associations that work well.

Whole-class discussions always impact the children socially. I feel it is my duty to give students an environment that is cooperative in nature, not isolating like the one I experienced when I was in school. Without a doubt, one of the most important functions a teacher can fulfill is helping children express their feelings and emotions, find ways to converse as they reveal what they are excited about or grappling with, and feel safe when they try to answer questions or ask for assistance. One of the ways to do this is by modeling small-group conversations in front of the whole class: as the students practice a partner book-talk during a large group meeting, stop to discuss all of the salient points of that group experience. The children can discuss what parts of the conversation were helpful, what was unnecessary, what they could try next time to reach more depth in their dialogue, and how each person felt as they were involved in the talk. By having the children notice what works well for partners, they begin to realize ways to increase their own discussion skills. Also, noting that good book talks can still have some parts that are not so useful allows students to see that it's okay to make mistakes, and that they can keep trying. And making them aware of new things to try gives them a chance to stretch their future work. Continuously bringing up feelings and attitudes sets the tone for becoming aware of emotions as something to look out for during any activity.

As I listed in the benefits of groups earlier (pages 11–13), working together gives children a chance to learn about and appreciate each other. They can best do this by being placed in mutually satisfying situations. When children are mingled in different grouping situations, they get to hear what *everyone* is thinking. In a group of three to five math investigators, when each child has a role and each child gets to do something well, the students can recognize each others' strengths. During small group work, such as a partner portrait-drawing project, students see the differences and similarities that are inherent in all of us.

I want children to feel comfortable in my class, even if they are experiencing sadness, confusion, anger, doubt, or worry. Having some established groups, such as learning center groups (see Chapter 2), allows for long-term, consistent work situations. As students get more familiar with those in their group, they are more willing to take academic and social risks. Children are more comfortable showing their emotions to someone they have spent a lot of time with. Group members also learn how to comfort each other, as well as help each other complete given tasks.

A community of learning

I also want students to share their feelings when they are curious, knowledgeable, enthusiastic, or dedicated. Because students get to know each other so well, they often come in with ideas and suggestions for free time or recess projects. By widening their circle of friends through work, these kids often invite others to join in their projects. During an activity, such as planting seeds, there will often be one child who gets very excited based on prior experiences. Make sure to partner a child like this with someone who is not as eager, so that the first child can help to spark interest and give information to the second child.

Encourage your students to tell each other when they are elated, triumphant, excited, or proud. During our many community-building discussions with the whole class, I ask students to take turns talking about why they are feeling these positive emotions. When they are

A Trip To Australia

I remember the year that one student, Adam, was going through a rough time at home and in school. He was in an extreme state of fury and frustration over recent changes in his family. Adam didn't know how to cope with it. He often ran out of the room, yelled at other students, curled up into a ball and wouldn't move; he got very little work or play done. I tried several ways to help him talk and work positively and productively. He was entitled to his feelings, but I knew that I needed to help him channel them. I chose Alexander and the Terrible, Horrible, No Good, Very Bad Day by Judith Viorst for a class read-aloud. In the book, Alexander wants to go to Australia when he is perturbed. We all had a long discussion about what we do when we are upset at home and what we could do when we're upset in school.

I cleared out some chairs from a table in the back of the room and told my class that we were going to make our very own "Australia" under that table. I asked the students how we should use our Australia and how we should decorate it. They decided that it would be a place where students could go if they needed a break. It was not somewhere that I could send a child for a time out. They also told me that if I was concerned about a student, I was permitted to suggest a trip to Australia, but I couldn't demand it.

The students worked on decorations in groups of four. I knew that I wanted to have a few children working together for two main reasons. First, I set up the activity as group work so that the students could start opening up about their feelings as they worked. They needed some other students present to start talking about what they do when they are frustrated. Second, I knew it was important for Adam to have a chance to bond with someone, and I wanted to give him some choices. I had seen him play with Charlie, Petey, and Dyan in the past, so I chose them to be in Adam's group of four. The students looked in books, then drew pictures of koalas and palm trees, kangaroos and rocks, water and grass. They made a big Australia label, and together we made a whole mural of things "Australian" against the wall below that table. We put books, paper, and crayons in a basket and placed that basket in our Australia. Adam ended up making five different pictures with his group to put under there—the most work he had produced at any one time in many weeks. He came in the next day with some shells from home. I felt a glimmer of hope.

As soon as we had our grand opening, Adam started making trips to Australia. The first few days he spent a lot of time there. At first, the other children would not go there if Adam was already there. As time passed, some would join him (Australia had a space limit of four kids). Petey, who worked with Adam on his pictures, began joining him there often, especially if he saw that Adam was agitated. I would frequently see them whispering. Then, slowly but surely, Adam started to visit Australia less and less. He and Petey became best friends, doing a lot of projects together and spending every recess with each other. Adam felt safe knowing that he had a place to go to if he needed it. He would not get in trouble, he would not upset the other students, and he would be able to calm down. He also had someone to talk to. Soon enough, Adam wanted to join in on our class projects. He wanted to be with other children out in the open, especially Petey. After they began to form their friendship, I let Adam and Petey be line partners, put them in the same reading group, and had them sit at the same table during work times. Of course, I made sure that both students had experiences with others, too. Still, Adam and Petey had created a special partnership of their own because they had seen and been a part of so many group experiences together throughout the year. I know that Australia, along with other interventions, had given Adam the confidence and control to be with the entire class more often. Petey was a big part of it, too! The success of working in groups while still having each other as an anchor gave both children the chance to grow and change.

working in small groups, I reinforce those discussions by asking children to tell their group what they are feeling good about. Children are also required to tell the group members what they thought the others did well. Providing students with the opportunity to work with their peers in a variety of settings helps them do all of these things because they internalize the questions, comments, and routines, and because they feel safe and accepted.

A Recipe for Successful Groupings

How can you be sure that your group work will be successful? Preparation is an essential element. Obviously groups cannot function without your direction and preparation. Deciding on goals and lessons, selecting materials, and devising group assignments is a bit like cooking. You need to plan ahead in order to mix up the class just right. If you do, your instruction and your students' work will result in a great "meal"!

A RECIPE FOR GROUP INSTRUCTION

- ✤ Get your ingredients (**decide subject, main idea, particular lesson**)
- ✤ Arrange your utensils (**materials, books, or worksheets**)
- ✤ Put contents in a bowl (**motivate students; explain the big picture—the "WHY?"**)
- ✤ Double check your recipe (**discuss the project and tasks with the class**)
- ✤ Mix and spoon out your batter (**organize your kids into groups**)
- ✤ Put the batter in the oven (**send the class off to work**)
- ✤ Stir occasionally (**check in with and help different groups**)
- ✤ Do a taste test (**see if the project is working for most or all of the class**)
- ✤ Remove from the oven (**gather the students back together**)
- ✤ Serve your meal (**share the results of the lesson**)
- ✤ Relax with dessert (**assess and plan for the future**)

It Takes Time

Bear in mind that productive group work doesn't just happen. In the beginning, a teacher spends a lot of time modeling good partnerships and group work. But after a month or so of experiencing this kind of extensive modeling and practice, students start to take pride in how they work with each other.

As the weeks progress, I grow more confident that when I form groups, the exchanges will generally be on task and productive. I feel better knowing that I don't have to actively monitor or participate in every conversation and activity, so I can focus on individual students or partnerships while the rest of the class works effectively together. By giving the children a trusting, dependable, and safe place to interact and learn with each other, I am offering them a place in which they can flourish.

Our "Australia" project gave groups a chance to talk about feelings and form special bonds.

CHAPTER TWO

THE WAY THINGS WORK
Strategies Available for Grouping

A s teaching became more and more a part of who I am, not just what I do, I began to develop a repertoire of grouping possibilities. All the grouping strategies that I studied in college and observed cooperating teachers utilize while a student teacher, all those that I heard about from other professionals and in staff development workshops, and those that I was beginning to try out and develop with my own classes started to take shape in my mind. I noticed the ways that grouping worked—and didn't—and I began to understand the kinds of things I needed to be aware of as I grouped my students.

As with so many aspects of education, when it came to grouping, I realized that I would need to take what I knew, add new ideas and formats to that, and make my own decisions about what I believe works best for arranging groups academically and socially. Doing this helped me to develop the types of groups and partnership situations that I now set up and apply each school year. Just as a child's learning constantly evolves based on what he or she is exposed to and attempts, so has my own pedagogy evolved. While I still leave room for trying out new things, and make grouping determinations based on each year's specific children and curriculum, I now have a solid repertoire of grouping strategies that I can apply and adapt to give my students the best learning experiences possible.

According to Richard F. Elmore, "Students may be grouped flexibly according to the teacher's judgement about the most appropriate array of strengths and weaknesses for a particular task or subject matter," ("Getting To Scale With Good Educational Practice," *Harvard Educational Review* 66.1, 1996). I put this into practice in my own grouping decisions, and firmly believe that this idea should be the foundation of all grouping strategies.

A Pyramid of Grouping Possibilities

There are many permutations that can occur as I group children for various curriculum areas and assorted class routines. I start out by thinking of my class as a pyramid. The bottom layer is the whole group. I want many of our lessons and share times to take place with everyone present. This permits the students to listen to each other and to me at the same time. Each successive layer of the pyramid involves a smaller grouping, based on what the children will work on, how I believe they will learn best, and what I expect them to gain from the students they are exploring with. The top of the pyramid is the individual child. One of the things that I contemplate each year is how I will help all my students reach their potential. I believe that it is important for children to grow toward independence and interdependence, and that this is to be achieved by understanding how to work both with others and on their own.

The pyramid structure (which I detail and diagram on page 24) has provided the guiding framework for my grouping strategies. But first, here are some of the key purposes, concepts, and terms related to grouping.

Range of Purposes and Types of Groups

Whether you are setting up formal groupings or allowing children to choose their own informal groups, certain formats and arrangements work best for particular intents. Different groupings or partnerships can facilitate various academic, social, or emotional development—and teachers must keep the individual personalities and whole-class dynamics in mind when making grouping decisions. For formal grouping, focus on the instructional objectives that you have established; there are certain ways to bring children together so that these aims can be met. For more informal groups, you might decide to set up activities based on daily lesson or project mandates, or perhaps ask the students to choose their own partners. There is a great range of purposes for grouping, and a considerable variety of potential groupings available. In order to help you understand better how to match a particular grouping strategy with a purpose, below are listed the key grouping terms and relationships, highlighting critical definitions, attributes, and types of groups.

Understanding Grouping: Key Terms

Heterogeneous Groups

This is a group made up of children with diverse skill levels who will work together so they can help each other out, learn from each other, and share in providing the knowledge that gets an

assignment completed. Students utilize their own strengths, and each child recognizes his or her own value during group situations. Children solidify their knowledge base by sharing and thinking with others who are at different stages of understanding. Students see that all of their classmates can do some things very well, and that all of them have areas that they are still developing. I form heterogeneous groups by carefully planning to place children at different levels together.

Students at different levels can help each other out.

Homogeneous Groups

These are groups composed of children who are at a similar stages of academic awareness and

performance. Children are assembled for these experiences to make sure that they have others around who are on par with them. It is often necessary to teach lessons to a small group of children so that they can get the direct guidance they need for a specific task, so it is important to create groups with students who need to practice or learn the same things. Groups of this sort are beneficial for ongoing training in various curriculum areas, such as literature or math groups. Homogeneous groups give students a chance to study many subject areas with a teacher's assistance *and* the support of their peers.

Students with similar skills support each other and move their learning forward.

Skill-Specific and Small-Task Groups

Skill-specific groups are similar to homogeneous groups, but are formed for much shorter periods of time, sometimes for only one lesson. These groupings are best used to reinforce something that has been done as a whole class, but that a few children didn't grasp, or for teaching something you notice during individual conferences that a few students need to work on. For example: After a math lesson, it may become apparent that three children didn't master the particular strategy highlighted in the lesson, so it is necessary to pull them together as a team and explain the strategy again. Or perhaps writing conferences will show that four or five students don't know how to use periods in the right places. A teacher can gather those children together for few minutes to work on that specific issue.

The classroom teacher generally determines who will be placed in heterogeneous, homogeneous, and skill-specific groups. These groups may last for a whole year, for one area of study, or for one distinct lesson.

Interest-Based Groups

An interest-based group is formed for a unit in a curriculum area that students need to research. It is important for students to be excited about what they are studying, and to be settled into the activity with other children who are interested in the same thing. When students are actively engaged in a study, they will be able to think about it and learn about it at higher levels. Students usually pick whom they will be with for these kinds of projects, but teachers can sometimes form interest groups based on their prior knowledge of their students. And even if students select group members themselves, the teacher should limit the number of participants and give some specific guidelines to ensure that all groups stay on task. After students get started, they need to be monitored occasionally during their work times. Any necessary assistance can be provided, and possible grouping changes can be made as time goes by. Interest-based groups may study topics prescribed by the curriculum or those determined by a teacher. They may also extend to topics that the students want to delve into of their own accord.

Socialization and Friendship Groups

Socialization and friendship groups can be formed for work times and play times to give children new social possibilities. Some children assemble their own groups on various occasions. In any classroom, there are always some students who are quiet and shy, or boisterous and loud, and others who are friendly or melancholic, instigative or helpful, competitive or compliant. Some students have more than one of these qualities, and other personality traits as well. It's great for children to have a chance to frolic and interact with all kinds of children, even if they might not be initially drawn to them. The children can get to know each other better and can even help calm a grandstander down or draw a more timid student out. It is essential to think about arranging the students with children of differing dispositions each time any kind of group is formed for academics. In fact, sometimes groups need to be formed for the sole purpose of socialization.

Formal Groups

Formal groupings, which are determined by the teacher, are long term (for at least a period of weeks, if not months, or a whole school year). While these groups are somewhat flexible, based on changing needs and developments, the decisions about who will be a member in a formal group is carefully thought out in advance. They are dictated by curriculum areas to be

Formal groups learn to work collaboratively on a variety of topics throughout the year.

23

studied, and by the academic and social needs of the individual children in the class. The students not only learn about the subject area covered, but also develop the important habits necessary for working with others.

Informal Groups

These kinds of groups are those that a teacher builds to fit a specific goal, lesson, project, or social need. Informal gatherings are generally formed for one lesson or project. The teacher or the students can decide who the group members will be. Students have all sorts of experiences with each other, and the teacher gets to see how they interact and perform in a variety of situations. Such groupings are especially beneficial because the students get to practice their negotiation and collaboration skills in different contexts. There are some fun ways to randomize these groupings. Many of the things that children do require that they work with someone else, but don't always necessitate or even fit with formal groups that have already been determined.

Daily, weekly, and monthly planning and preparation help a teacher decide what is crucial for the students to practice. This is the time to determine whether the children will do a specific activity or unit independently, in a formal group that already exists, or in an informal group that can be pulled together for a project during a particular day or week.

Partnerships

Partnerships provide students with a chance to develop and build upon friendships and academic strategies. Whether partnerships are daily, short-term, or long-term, formally or informally grouped, children in a class need opportunities to work on a variety of subjects in the most intimate form of groupings so that they can gain the skills necessary to be successful in larger groupings. By working one on one, students help out and learn from each other as they are creating lifelong work habits.

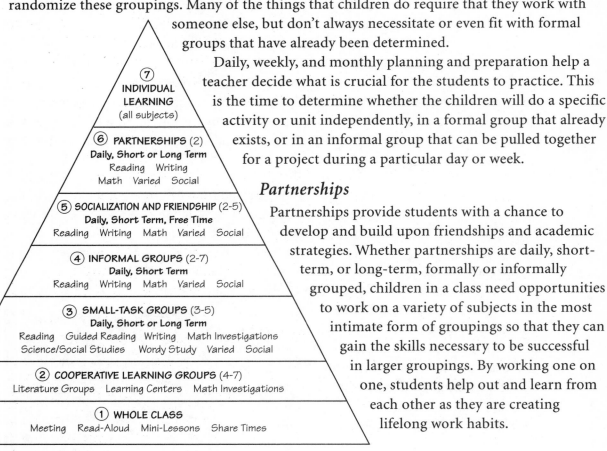

⑦ INDIVIDUAL LEARNING (all subjects)

⑥ PARTNERSHIPS (2)
Daily, Short or Long Term
Reading   Writing
Math   Varied   Social

⑤ SOCIALIZATION AND FRIENDSHIP (2-5)
Daily, Short Term, Free Time
Reading   Writing   Math   Varied   Social

④ INFORMAL GROUPS (2-7)
Daily, Short Term
Reading   Writing   Math   Varied   Social

③ SMALL-TASK GROUPS (3-5)
Daily, Short or Long Term
Reading   Guided Reading   Writing   Math Investigations
Science/Social Studies   Wordy Study   Varied   Social

② COOPERATIVE LEARNING GROUPS (4-7)
Literature Groups   Learning Centers   Math Investigations

① WHOLE CLASS
Meeting   Read-Aloud   Mini-Lessons   Share Times

Moving from Whole-Class to Group Formats to Individual Work

As I construct my planning for a school year, I use the ideas in this pyramid to help me determine what groupings I'll need to implement and enhance the experiences my students will have. Moving from the whole toward the individual, constantly interlacing smaller group formats, allows me to help my students reach their potential. I balance the ways that I create groups with the different grouping structures.

I developed the ideas in this pyramid of learning to allow for personal excellence as children figure out, with my guidance, how to be independent and interdependent. The progression of curricular explanation, information gathering, and knowledge sharing weaves through the different levels. All of the stages in the pyramid have tremendous value for educating children. While separate entities, the categories in the pyramid overlap for a variety of subjects and purposes.

The Whole Class

I start out the school year working most often with my whole class. I feel that it is vital to do many activities with everyone in attendance early on. As the year progresses, or after a whole-group discussion, I put smaller group situations into effect. The whole-class setting is the place for morning meeting, read-alouds, mini-lessons, and information sharing, all of which are described below.

Meetings

I start each day with a meeting that involves everyone. We gather each morning in a circle on our rug to discuss the day and to go over certain daily rituals and routines. Our morning meeting is a time where we get to say "hello," to discuss pertinent information, and to work on whole-group projects and tasks. Throughout the week, some of the things that we do as a class at meeting time are: sing a good morning song; share word work or journal review (one of which is the first activity the kids do as they filter into class in the morning); go over the day's schedule; discuss the day's message; talk about special events, holidays, or trips; do calendar work or the math problem of the day; count the number of days of school; talk about our poem of the week; and/or review homework. I may call a meeting at a different time in the school day if we have an issue or problem that comes up, or if it is warranted by the work we are doing. Of course, the morning meeting routines vary on different days of the week and at different times of the school year, but we are always together as a whole group.

Read-Alouds

I try to read aloud to my students as a whole class at least twice a day. I generally read a picture book or nonfiction book to my class before the students do Reading Workshop. The workshop can involve all aspects of balanced reading: independent reading, guided reading, partner reading, shared reading, book talk, reading response, or word study. I do this so that we can discuss an idea in the book, study the author's style, or work on a specific aspect of decoding or comprehension that I think will benefit every student in the class. I always send students off to read with a task (such as "Today I want you to see which words you figured out and how you did it," "Today you should make sure you know which character is talking," or "Today you should choose a new book written by an author you have read before").

The second time I read to my whole class each day is called "dessert" because reading is indeed so sweet, and because this usually occurs right after lunch/recess. Very often I read from a chapter book, and the books I choose fit in with some aspect of our curriculum. During dessert, I read for a longer period of time, stopping to ask many different kinds of factual, thought-provoking, and inferential questions. I invite the children to make predictions, and we discuss vocabulary words, talk about broad themes, and make connections between this book and other books or the students' own lives. I value this whole-class time because it can help solidify literacy learning, and because we can strengthen our community by sharing what we read and think.

Mini-Lessons

I often need to review or teach a new strategy before sending students off to work on a project or assignment. These mini-lessons are best done with the whole class on the rug and can involve all topic areas: reading, writing, math, science, social studies, word study, art, etc. I call the students together, and they either sit in a circle or gather in close to me. Mini-lessons usually run 10 to 15 minutes long, and afterwards I always send the students off with a task, whether they'll be working independently or with other children. It is important to start any undertaking with all of the children together, and then, when they are actively working, to support them in the areas or skills that they are ready for.

A MINI-LESSON CAN BE USED TO:
- Detail what the class will be doing
- Discuss the upcoming project
- Review prior concepts or work
- Plan the next activity
- Write out a chart story
- Do an interactive writing piece
- Fill out a graph, chart, or data table
- Collect information about the particular subject
- Choose groups for the upcoming lesson

Sharing

The whole class is also the best setting for students to share their experiences, learning, or discoveries. A "share" is the time for all of the children to discuss their strategies and understandings together. It's important for them to do this so that they can process whatever they are working on and gain ideas from each other. Although we do a mini-lesson before every activity, we do not have a share after every lesson. Often we'll discuss certain things as a part of the morning meeting instead of having a dedicated share time. However, we do have reading, writing, math, and content-area shares frequently. The students come together so that they can, for example, read their writing, talk about a math system, explain a decoding strategy, discuss a science investigation, and tell about what worked or didn't work. It's important to have whole-class shares after independent and group situations; these can be based on shared reading, chart-tablet stories, choral poetry, graphs, or other activities.

Cooperative Learning Groups

During a typical school year, I create some large groups (four to seven students) that will remain pretty much together throughout the year. I also arrange some bigger cooperative learning groups for specific projects that may last for several days, a few weeks, or even a few months. Almost without exception, I find that the level of my students' learning and performance is raised because they get to develop good working relationships with each other in these steady groups.

Sometimes these groups will be heterogeneous and based on ability or interest. The determining factor of how cooperative groups are formed stems from the aim for the group. In my class, the activities performed in these groups are interwoven throughout my weekly planning. Although the children occasionally have input about the make-up of groups of this size during play times or more casual activities, the membership choices are usually the teacher's. The selection of long-term, larger groups is extremely important and in most cases must be directed by the teacher, who understands the academic and social goals of the groupings as well as the skills and personalities of the individual members.

Literature Groups

One of the possible applications for cooperative learning groups is in the study of literature. After assessing the reading abilities of individual students, you can organize them into literature groups for shared book experiences throughout the year. These groups are usually composed of four or five children who exhibit comparable skills in their reading decoding and comprehension. I work with each group about once every week or so. I also train parents and student teachers to work with each group. Generally, the students are reading from books at their independent level. With modeling and the support of an adult who asks the right questions and stops at pertinent points in the book, students begin to internalize the kinds of questions they need to ask themselves and the places they should stop and think.

Once a group is stable, the students may read independently once in a while from the same book, and then come together for discussions. While these groups last for the whole school year, each child's placement is adaptable. Students may be moved into different groups if their competency exceeds other children in their group, or if they need more assistance. Personally— and professionally—I love literature groups because they give children a chance to think and talk deeply about their common reading experiences more informally than in our "dessert" books discussions. The children in literature groups become adept at helping each other sound out words, interpret information, and think deeply about fiction and nonfiction books.

Learning Centers

Learning centers also involve grouping a large number of children together. I sort my students into four groups, usually seven in each (as I usually have about 28 students each year). Every week I plan four lessons that will get done during learning center sessions. My student teachers (or sometimes parents) and I will monitor learning center activities. This is a terrific format for both interdependent and directed study. On a day in which my lesson plan features learning center activities, the groups visit one center for 30 to 35 minutes to do a lesson. We rotate the groups four times during that school day, so that by the end of the day each group has worked with an adult and completed every activity. When I don't have enough adults, I plan independent centers in which the children can manage the task alone. We do learning centers once a week, and I form new groups mid-year.

Learning center work is the crux of content-area teaching in my class. The class visits social studies and science lessons each week, and other centers can focus on writing, math, reading, art, games, puzzles, word work, handwriting, projects, cooking, and so on. The learning center format allows us to connect curriculum areas and to study in an interdisciplinary manner. More often than not, all four centers revolve around a specific theme, such as researching an inventor: reading, writing, doing one of their experiments, and making a model of an invention.

I carefully make each learning center group heterogeneous. It's important to put a strong reader, writer, talker, artist, and mathematician in each group. Shy children are placed in a group with someone who might become a friend. I also arrange members so that there are only one or two children with special learning or behavior needs in each group, and children who distract each other or who are very best friends are placed in different groups. I may sometimes need to balance

Learning centers allow for interdependent, independent, and assisted study.

the groups by grade (I generally teach a bridge class with a two-grade span) and gender. Though the groupings usually work well and stay together each semester, if there are any problems, a switch will be made before new learning centers groups are devised in February. I occasionally use the learning center groups during other school events because it's a quick and easy way to sort my class. I can assemble the students into learning center groups for a class trip, projects with a cluster teacher, or if I want to work on a topic with a smaller number of children.

The learning centers are also a terrific tool for teachers, allowing them to plan wonderful experiments and lessons that would be too hard to manage with the whole class. Instead, students have a quiet, focused group to learn with, and all the children get a chance to participate and to talk to each other. And learning center groups allow teachers to work with all of their students in a given subject area—all in one day!

I find that hanging a sign or poster in the room listing the various group members makes group work easier to manage and helps foster that sense of team work that I am trying to build among my students. At right is a typical learning center group sign that I will print and hang up near each center's activity cards. The group titles always relate to a unit of study.

After switching the learning center groups this year, I asked my students to talk about what they thought of working in learning centers. I wanted the children to

LEARNING CENTERS GROUPS	
RADIO	**TELEVISION**
EZRA	CAROL
FRANK	GUY
HALLIE	JAKOB
JEN	KEVIN
JOHNNY	KINARI
JORDAN	LUCAS
LENA	MOLLY
LAUREN	
COMPUTER	**SATELLITE**
ANNA	BENNY
CONOR	DORIE
DAVID	JAHBARI
DAYNA	JESSE
DUNCAN	RYDER
DYLAN	SHAIYA
SAMANTHA	SAGE

have a chance to discuss their experiences. This is what some of them said:

WHAT DO YOU LIKE ABOUT LEARNING CENTERS?

Lucas: *I like that I have a good group to look forward to.*

Sage: *If you need help, you can ask someone in your group.*

Jesse: *In your group, you get to have at least one good friend.*

Shaiya: *I like learning centers because you get to learn more about new stuff with your friends.*

Ryder: *We get to see some people we don't usually see when we do stuff in class.*

Frank: *I like learning centers because it's not only with kids, you get to know grown-ups too.*

Hallie: *You don't have to figure things out by yourself. You can figure it out with your group.*

Duncan: *After a while, you get to be friends with everyone in your group.*

TEACHER'S TAKE: It is always helpful for me to know what is working and what needs improvement in any of the grouping situations I arrange. By asking students to tell me what they like about learning centers, I can make plans for the formation of new groups and for future lessons. And I am always thrilled that many of my students recognize and find good things to say about learning centers based on what they've done during the previous months.

Math Investigations

Groups of four to seven children work well for some math investigations. I usually form these groups during certain mathematical area inquiries; they last for the duration of the investigation, not for a whole school year. First, I gather the groups together to investigate materials or a problem. They will be directed to think something through and to take notes or create a chart to show their outcomes. While I frequently form math groups of two to three children, I think a math group should consist of more (four to seven) when any of the following things apply:

- An investigation requires a lot of sorting and figuring

- We are nearing the end of a unit and the children are ready to make broader connections

- A few students need the support of stronger mathematicians

- Most of my children are working in partnerships, but there are a few students who need a challenging problem, or a few students who need teacher intervention

- The math work involves more complicated organizing or cumbersome building

Small-Task, Skill-Specific, or Study Groups

Students will often work in smaller groups for short periods of time. These small-task groups are set up to do particular explorations or studies that require a few heads or hands working together. The students sometimes get to pick which classmates they will work with, if the activity is interest-based or an open-ended game that allows for different levels of learning. However, teachers should choose the group members if they feel that their students need to work with someone on their level for that skill or if they want to arrange the groups so that children with a strength in a certain area support the others. Small-task groups can be utilized in all curriculum areas.

Reading and Guided Reading

A balanced reading program requires the students to have opportunities to listen to, read closely, write about, and discuss many genres within the contexts of fiction and nonfiction books. The children will work together and/or with the teacher on books, articles, poems, author or genre studies, word study activities, parts of speech, and other things that relate to reading fluency and understanding.

During reading, three or four students who are reading the same genre, author, or book series will do a study. As a group, they'll read together, ask each other questions, take notes, and generally share their reflections about the genre, author, or series. Even during read together times, the children sometimes form their own little groups just because they want to.

Guided-reading groups (skill-specific groupings) fall under this category as well. As you read with and assess your students during independent and partner reading, make note of things that each needs to practice in all reading areas, such as inferring, sounding out words, using context clues, and character understanding. You can then call together students who need to work on the same strategy. Periodically, I will do an extremely focused lesson for 15 or 20 minutes to target that reading need using an instructional-level text, and each child in my class is involved in at least one guided-reading group during most weeks. These groups differ from literature groups because they do not have stable members and do not last for any length of time. The purpose here is to help the children internalize the specific strategy we work on together, so that it becomes a part of their reading repertoire.

Learning From Real Life

Sometimes It Happens Naturally

A couple of years ago I had a few students who were obsessed with The Bailey School Kids *series of books. The five children in this self-initiated group got together to read and write about what they were learning. Each of them read a different book from the series every day, even taking the books with them to recess. They talked about the stories incessantly. There was always one child or another running up to me to tell about what was happening in a book, letting me in on predictions, or comparing his or her book to someone else's. The group compiled a list of the four main characters, including personality descriptions, lists of the characters' likes and dislikes, and details about their adventures. Each child did a character map for the other (non-recurring) main character in* The Bailey School Kids *book he or she had read. Then all of the students together wrote an essay detailing the similarities and differences in the five books. The kinds of conversations they had with each other and the kinds of writing they did about the series were deepened because they became a group of* The Bailey School Kids *lovers!*

Study groups are short term, too. Children who have an interest in a particular genre or author will get together for a few days or weeks to read books and make connections about that genre or author's style. The students need to do a project or write about the things they learn when they are in a study group. They often get to choose their group members, with some guidance from the teacher. Sometimes the entire class will break off into study groups they initiate themselves; at other times, one or two sets of students may work in groups while other students do a larger group study or work independently as the teacher does conferences.

In my classroom, I organize reading centers at different points during a school year with a handful of activities that the students rotate through (similar to the learning centers described earlier). The reading centers involve buddy reading, word study, reading response, and the like. When I set up reading centers, I group students for the duration of that center cycle, and the groups are usually heterogeneous.

Writing

Writing experiences with groups of this size—about three to five students—work best if the members are helping each other revise or edit their pieces. Children who are working on the same kinds of stories can also sit together to help each other out. When children have a chance to talk through what they are writing about, it helps them add greater depth to their characters and plots. Partnerships are also a good format for revision and editing tasks.

It's also a good idea to have students create an editing checklist to use as they work with their group. This helps keep the editing process focused. In the example below, we all decided on—after a long discussion—the components of a good piece of writing, and then developed this series of questions for writers and their partners to ask themselves. We listed them in order of importance.

ACCOUNTABLE WRITING: Student Checklist

When you revise/edit your writing with a partner, use these question to check your writing.

___ Does it make sense?

___ Does the writer use detailed information?

___ Does it tell the whole story?

___ Does it have a beginning, a middle, and an ending?

___ Does the writer use interesting, descriptive language?

___ Does the writing have a strong lead and finish?

___ Are there spaces between the words?

___ Does it seem that the writer used good spelling and sounding out strategies?

___ Does it have appropriate punctuation?

___ Are upper- and lower-case letters used correctly?

___ Does it have clear handwriting and a neat presentation?

___ Are there detailed illustrations?

When three of my students were editing some stories, I was fortunate enough to overhear part of their conversation:

Group Work in Action

HELPING WITHOUT TAKING OVER

Dolly: *I'm ready to edit for periods, but I'm not sure where to put them all.*

Jose: *Read it to us, and we'll listen to where your voice stops.*

Dolly: *Why don't you read it first so you'll get it better?*

Marilyn: *Cool. Jose, I'll read it to both of us. Dolly, stay close, in case we need help.*

After Marilyn read the writing aloud, it was Dolly's turn to read to her partners.

Marilyn: *Stop. You need a period right after the word "friends."*

(Dolly continues to read.)

Jose: *Stop. I think you should put an exclamation point after "excited."*

Marilyn: *Good one.*

(Dolly reads on.)

Marilyn: *Stop. Put a period there.*

Jose: *No, you need a question mark. You're asking for an answer.*

Marilyn: *Oh, you're right.*

Roe: *I heard some of what you were saying to each other. I love the way you're helping Dolly edit her work. You three make a good team because none of you takes over. I can tell that you realize you need to help Dolly see where punctuation goes. No one did it for her. Later on she'll be able to do it herself!*

TEACHER'S TAKE: The kids continued on like this until the work was completed. I wanted to interject what I noticed so that I could name for them what they were doing in the hopes that they would repeat that type of wonderful assistance in future efforts. I loved how they supported Dolly without doing it for her. This one exchange may have helped Dolly to hear her own "stops" independently. This is the kind of natural assistance that I would later discuss with the whole class.

Writing centers are devised along the lines of learning and reading centers and generally last a week or so. Determinations about which children will work together lean toward homogeneous grouping. Occasionally, I set up a variety of activities geared to elevate the level of my student's writing skills, and I have the children rotate through each of the centers, staying with their group, until they have completed all activities. Writing centers are particularly helpful when there are several students who need to work on the same kinds of things. The activities might be poetry writing, story writing, word work, editing, writing-skills worksheets, and so on.

Math Investigations

Math investigations are great for this smaller number of students. My students use a lot of manipulatives for our hands-on math work, so when three, four, or five students work together, they can sort materials and concepts faster, can help each other categorize, and can figure out problems by combining their thoughts and strategies. It really benefits students to work in groups when a multi-step math equation is presented to them in a word problem or using data that needs to be sorted and classified. Children can share their mathematical knowledge and build on what the students in their group already know.

Each member of this problem-solving trio contributes thoughts and strategies to figure out a math word problem.

I plan for groups of "math problem solvers" when my students will be working on an investigation that will take a few days. The students might be figuring out all the ways to make rectangles (arrays) using tiles, or they may have a difficult word problem to decipher. Problem-solving groups are comprised of four or five children with a comparable facility for mathematics. I decide who works together for these short-term gatherings. This way, I know that the students are on the same level and will be able to learn from each other without anyone lagging behind. It is also easier for me to assign appropriate problems when the students have similar skills.

During many school years, I attach a "Graph of the Week" on the door of my classroom, which the students fill out on their own when they have a free moment. I vary the graphs so the children have an opportunity to do bar graphs, circle graphs, pie charts, Venn diagrams, t-charts, and other kinds of data representations as the school year progresses. Frequently, I'll select specific, small groups of children to look at the graph in the middle of each week to see if there are noticeable patterns or to figure out answers to some of the guiding questions. This is a chance to have three or four students practice what they need to, if they happen to be grappling with the issues presented by the graph we are working on. I may also group a few students who have stronger graphing skills to take 20 minutes or so to complete a graph. The whole class reviews these graphs at the end of each week, incorporating them into a math lesson for the concept we are studying at the time.

Science and Social Studies Mini-Units

I often set up science and social studies mini-units in which students do things like magnet experiments, planting, map reading and making, or studying a city or country. These mini-unit activities offer a perfect situation to let students decide on their group members, since skill level and background knowledge can be combined. It's also great to have a few children in a mini-unit group so that they can really help each other out with procedures and observations.

We work in groups of "explorers" and "investigators" when my lesson plans call for a study that involves a lot of reading and writing. Explorers research and record facts usually related to social studies ideas. Investigators find data and do experiments often involving science inquiries. We do these projects using classroom and outside resources when I want students to take ownership of learning whole concepts. The students are grouped heterogeneously, so that

The Power of Common Interests

Hallie, Lena, and Jahbari were not students I ever would have imagined playing together. They were very pleasant to each other, but had different friends and divergent interests. When the class received an assignment to pick something about electricity that they wanted to learn more about, these three children all decided that they wanted to know how light switches worked. Once they sat down together, I could see that they were having a hard time getting a conversation started to determine their next steps. I came over with a few science books that had information they needed, asked them a few guiding questions about light switches, and moved away. Within minutes, they had decided to take turns reading the same books, or sections of books. Two days later, during research time, I checked back in with the group. I found out that they had set up a working play-date at Lena's house for that Saturday. The children had already devised a list of who would do what to build their own electrical circuit so that they could see how a light switch works. Their initial discomfort with working together was overcome once they focused on a subject that interested all of them and the specific task at hand.

they can share their strengths and ideas, expanding their knowledge. The groups last for the duration of the study. Students really enjoy these projects because most children are fascinated by the world and how it works. The combination of studying those things and working with friends is very compelling.

Science and social studies activities are also woven into many of the things that our class does. Throughout the year, we read numerous nonfiction science and history books, along with books that have facts mixed in with made-up characters, (as in *The Magic School Bus* series). When we write nonfiction pieces, they tie into the experiments we are doing and the things we are studying about the world. I usually plan a year-long social studies theme that I link to science. For example, when we studied New York City one year, we learned about and visited all five boroughs. We explored the different ethnic groups living in the city and did a lot of map-making for social studies. As a link to science, we investigated New York City's water system, sewer system, seasons, electricity, and indigenous plants and animals. When the class was doing an examination of how electricity works, three children who were in a group planned play-dates and talked on the phone every night to discuss the project, even though the work was getting done in school. This is a testament to their dedication as investigators, and to the benefits of having children work as a group. Indeed, working on these activities in groups made the children's understandings— and the project outcomes—richer because of the collaboration of ideas, knowledge, and personalities.

Word Study and Spelling

Small task groups are a particularly effective format for doing word-study inquiries (phonics). The students can choose their group members because their different background knowledge of phonics can help strengthen each child's work. They also get to work with friends so they are more likely to be motivated. For example, in order to investigate the various concepts of how the English language works, I have students use books, dictionaries, and encyclopedias to look for words, parts of speech, spelling rules, and irregular word examples. As the school year goes on, I ask them to search for and write down words with a *gr* blend at the beginning, *-ing* suffix words, plurals that don't have an *s*, adjectives, adverbs, and so forth. The students congregate all over the room using the sources available to help each other find as many words as possible that fit the conventions I've asked them to explore. I can always tell who has worked with whom because they always make sure that all of their partners have the same words on their list.

During word-study activities, students often form their own groups. This occurs naturally, because they understand what the assignment is and because they quickly learn how beneficial it is to work with others. During investigations of some of the more difficult word-study concepts, (such as when to double a final consonant, or understanding how to write words with vowel combinations), I will form groups of a few students with the same word-study or spelling needs. This allows me to do some targeted work with the group, and enables students to support each other as they are grappling with the ideas involved in the study.

"Words in Words" is an activity my students love to do. I hang up a chart with a title on top. The students get to hunt for words that they can make using the letters in the title. For example, if the title is *Winter is Cold*, students can write *on, low, sit, tire, tired, old, sold, told*, and so on. The chart is displayed in a place where the kids can easily work on it if they have free time or have finished their current assignment. The students generally pair themselves off, but I will sometimes ask a child who needs more spelling practice to work with students who are better spellers.

Here is a poem I wrote for a class during a word study on contractions. I knew that it would help as we discussed how to "put words together":

PUT TOGETHER

Would've, should've, could've;
things I think about!

Won't, can't, don't;
things that leave me with doubt!

I'll, you'll, we'll;
let's work together!

Isn't, hasn't, wasn't;
our play in any weather!

Put together words,
Put together friends,

Put together learning,
Bringing you to new ends!

Informal, Lesson- or Project-Based Groups

While many of the grouping possibilities that are arranged for students are based on decisions made by the teacher, by curriculum mandates, and by best-work practices, the nature of groupings can also be very informal. Often when students are given assignments with no grouping instructions, groups nevertheless occur. Students will gravitate towards each other naturally, of their own accord. And lesson- or project-based groups that arise in such a manner are just as meaningful and useful as if a teacher had decided to form groups.

Students sometimes work in groups of two to seven in this informal way. Let students group themselves for an exploration or game, or for an art project if they like. You might even create an impromptu group if the class will be working on research reports for a few weeks, if they are doing something like sorting or graphing data, or if you want to study an author with specific children.

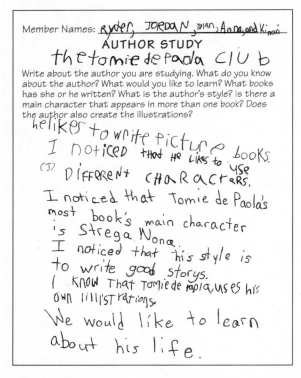

Member Names: Ryder, JORDAN, Dylan, Anna, and Kinari
AUTHOR STUDY
the tomie de Paola CIUb

Write about the author you are studying. What do you know about the author? What would you like to learn? What books has she or he written? What is the author's style? Is there a main character that appears in more than one book? Does the author also create the illustrations?

he likes to write picture books.
I noticed that he likes to use
(J) Different characters.
I noticed that Tomie de Paola's
most book's main character
is Strega Nona.
I noticed that his style is
to write good storys.
I know that Tomie de Paola uses his own lillistrations.
We would like to learn about his life.

AUTHOR STUDY GROUPS

Tomie De Paola
Anna, Ryder, Dylan, Kinari, Jordan

Dr. Seuss
Hallie, Molly, Guy, Lena, Carol

Patricia Polacco
Ezra, Dorie, Samantha, Datna

Bill Cosby
Benny, Conor, Shaiya, Sage

Syd Hoff
Jesse, Jakob

Cynthia Rylant
Duncan, Frank, David, Johnny

Eloise Greenfield
Lauren, Jen

Ezra Jack Keats
Lucas, Kevin, Jahbari

These informal groups can happen more or less often, depending on time factors, class needs, and other academic variables. I really like this grouping strategy because it gives me a chance to see who the students choose to work with (or not to work with), and how they interact with children they may not spend too much time with. The free-flowing nature of these groups is very motivational.

Grouping students is something that permeates all that happens in my classroom. The overall question that I keep in mind during any planning that involves or may involve group work is: "Who gets to choose the group members and why?"

Teacher-Determined Groups

All teacher-determined groupings are crucial. Groups that last for a whole year or half a year support the learning that takes place for academic subjects. Shorter and more casual groupings that teachers decide on are used for specific goals revolving around key issues and target skills. In order for children to form their own groups, to learn how to work, and to practice the topics they need to independently, they must first learn how to work well with others. This learning takes place with the assistance of a teacher who forms groups based on what she knows about her students.

If you have specific goals for long-term, short-term, and informal groups, then you decide which children will work together. You will make the decisions about group formats and members by balancing your knowledge of what each child understands, what he or she needs to learn next, how he or she can best be supported in the work, and what social aims are also at hand.

There are many times when the students in my class are learning with a group or partner on a multi-disciplinary project. During most inquiries or studies, the children need to read, do research, take notes, write essays or responses, create a chart or graph, do an art project, and present or display their findings. I have to consider all of the different work disciplines involved, how the students will interact for projects of this sort, and all of the grouping strategies available when determining who should work together.

Student-Determined Groups

There are many kinds of activities that take place in different academic subjects that allow for children to work together, but do not mandate any specific grouping. These casual lessons are times when children can choose to work with whomever they'd like. There are also times when motivation and comfort are essential elements for students to be able to navigate an academic or social experience—so whom they get to work with can affect their results.

Students generally get to make their own decisions about group members during these more informal experiences. Also, if an activity can be performed either independently or with others, students can have more of a say in how they will do that activity. Let the students make the decisions when you want to reinforce the excitement of a project or when you want the students to become more engaged. Giving the children some control of how and with whom they'll work allows them to be full members of the classroom community.

As students become more proficient at working with others and at having meaningful, on-task discussions, let them make group choices more often. The ability to make good grouping decisions is one of the things that is assisted by your earlier group choices, by a good deal of grouping practice, and by many whole-class discussions on the group experiences that the students have had. You can actually gauge the progress towards independence that your students are making by their success at choosing their own group members for different projects and lessons.

Informal groups give children an opportunity to learn how to make good grouping decisions on their own.

Socialization and Friendship

While academic achievement and excellence is clearly the main objective in any classroom, friendships and social/emotional growth are significant aims as well. We all live and learn better when we do things surrounded by people we care about—and who care about us.

Children develop friendships naturally and play and work with those with whom they already feel comfortable. By incorporating teacher- and student-determined groupings into your classroom, you can actually increase the friendships and social experiences that your students have in school. The more occasions to work with and learn about others that students have, the wider their circle of friends becomes—and the richer their knowledge and experiences will be. When students interact with each other in many different ways, they learn things about their world more deeply and profoundly. The informal lessons and projects that occur during any school year provide a welcome opportunity for my students to work with those they are already friendly with, and to become friends with new children.

When my class was doing science note-taking in order to create a research report, I let the students decide if they would work alone or with someone else. The assignment was to become an "IST" (as in *scientist*). I wanted them to study the various kinds of presentations, data, statistics, and so forth included in nonfiction books; the tools that scientists use; and the information required to explain a subject. Ezra and Sage resolved to become meteorologists because they both wanted to use the same book. They chose to work together, even though they hadn't spent a lot of time with each other prior to this assignment, simply because of the materials available. As they were doing research, this is what I overheard.

BUILDING FRIENDSHIPS WHILE LEARNING

Ezra: *Is it my turn or your turn?*

Sage: *Mine.*

Ezra: *Okay, but we still don't know what kind of cloud that is.*

Sage: *I'll read it and tell you about it.*

Ezra: *I don't understand. What page is that?*

Sage: *All right. Wait, let me read it to you.*

Ezra: *You hold the book, and I'll write the notes.*

TEACHER'S TAKE: The children built up a friendship, starting with a common interest (meteorology) and a mutual need (the science book). Ezra and Sage informally went about creating a group for a project, with very little teacher input. They found ways to help each other, to learn new things, and to get along. I could see that prior group experiences guided them toward successful collaboration. Since both children were absorbed in the topic and the project, they enthusiastically worked together to get things done.

Partnerships

Over the years, I have found that stable partnerships in different curriculum areas are the heart of teaching kids to discover together. Partnerships are always made up of two students. If I have an odd number of children in my class, or if someone needs a lot of support, I will set up a three-member partnership. Each school year, I make sure that the students have a strong, lasting partnership in either reading, writing, or math. While this partnership helps the particular task get completed, it also helps the children gain the social and emotional understanding necessary for success in larger groups. I only do one or two of these formal associations in any given year because I feel it would be too confusing to have them in all three main subject areas. I begin partnerships early in the school year, before any larger groups are formed, so that the students can "rehearse" talking and working with others.

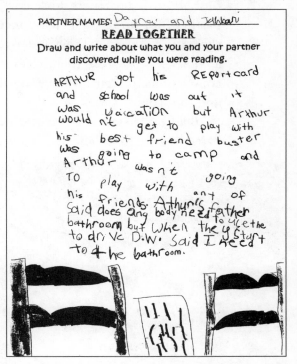

Students who wouldn't naturally work together can and do learn from each other while enjoying a new partnership.

Partnerships for Reading

When I set up formal reading partners, I first let the students "try out" different classmates. I observe and read with them, and then I make the ultimate decision based on skills (which doesn't necessarily mean kids have to be at the same skill level), or on children who may need a partner to draw them out or keep them on task. However, reading partners are generally on or close to the same level of decoding expertise and comprehension. The partners will be assigned the same book, books by the same author, or a book in the same genre. These book decisions are determined by the other things we are studying in class as the year progresses. Reading partners read together twice a week and independently twice a week. This allows them to vary their read-aloud and silent-reading experiences and to practice all kinds of good reading strategies.

Learning From Real Life

Partnerships Help Learning

I sometimes put my students into partnerships with children they would not likely choose on their own. Initially, there is a certain amount of grumbling and face-making, but that usually vanishes quickly. One good example is the time my students had to read together and then write and draw about what they read. Some students clearly would have preferred a different partner than the one I assigned, but by the time they had their books and were reading, every single child was into it! After the activity was done, I asked the class how it was to work with someone new. They all said that it was "fun," "exciting," "great," "cool," and so on! The work they produced was superb. And I loved the way that all of their personalities came through in their writing and art.

Book talk is a regular feature in my classroom. During years in which I assign students permanent reading partners, they do book talks with their partners. If we have not established formal reading partners, I use one of the informal grouping strategies to let children choose a partner for a book talk at least once a week. A book talk encourages children to converse with each other to deepen their understanding of a book. In these partnerships, students can discuss a book they have read themselves or one I have read to the class. Their discussions can make connections to their own lives or other books, or they can investigate characters, plots, genres, and so forth.

Book buddies are a more flexible, temporary form of reading partnership. Students work in pairs, but the "buddies" do not need to have similar reading skills. In fact, it is often preferable for the students to have different abilities so that they can support and help one another as they delve into books. Since I frequently teach bridge classes, I'll sometimes even set up book buddies with students from an older or younger class. Paired with older students, my younger students learn new things, and when older students read with younger students, they solidify their own skills. Intra-class book buddies allows for building a larger community of friends and learners, too!

Writing partners are enthusiastic supporters and diligent editors of each other's work.

Partnerships for Writing

Writing partnerships do not have to be as analogous as reading partnerships. When students have lasting partnerships for writing, they can support each other in many ways, so their specific proficiencies are not as important. When the pairs are established, the children have an opportunity to get to know each other's habits and ideas in depth. It will prove extremely beneficial to use established writing partners in those years when you feel that your students need this kind of dedicated support in addition to the usual writing projects and discussions that take place over time. When writing, the partners should always sit near each other, even if they are doing independent work. This way, they may easily check in with each other at any time during writing (and without disturbing the other children).

Writing partners always revise content and edit concepts of print together and help each other out with ideas, details, comments, questions, and skills. And such circumstances have the added benefit of allowing students who are strong speakers to feel good about themselves even if they're not fluent writers. The students really get to know each other's sense of story, character development, and qualities of expression. The partnerships also allow children to collaborate on stories and, boy, do they come up with some great ideas! A few years ago, two of my students, Matthew and Andy, created a series of books on "Super Cookie" and "Super Oreo." They used those characters throughout the entire year in different kinds of writing pieces. Everyone from that class still remembers the "Super Team."

Writing partners work together less often and with no specific format dictated by me. If these are not formally established, year- or semester-long pairings, I let the children choose their buddies during certain studies, such as when we are doing character story writing. These are generally not long-term partnerships (just for the duration of a project or lesson), since I want the children to have experiences with others.

For example, prior to one writing project, we had read a lot of books with strong main characters such as "Nate The Great," "Junie B. Jones," "Julian" from the Julian Stories, "Cam Jansen," and the "Henry and Mudge" series. The assignment was for each child to select one of those main characters and write a new adventure for him or her. One group formed based on a shared desire to pen a new plot for Nate the Great.

Collaborators work on writing stories together. There are occasions when I want the whole class to write in teams, usually when I want everyone to focus more on thinking through a story, adding details, and/or expanding their use of descriptive language. When this happens, I start out by having the kids discuss their ideas with the class and then pair off with whomever they want to write. I negotiate the final partnerships for kids who don't have an idea or don't have anyone with whom to work.

Creating the "Super Team" allowed Mathew and Andy to practice many new writing strategies with each other all year long.

Partnerships for Editing

Partnerships for editing and revising are extremely helpful. The students will often discuss story concepts together or ask each other for help with spelling, each and every day. They quickly learn who has great topic ideas, who can help with dialogue, and who spells really well. When students are working on revising or editing a piece for a publishing party or for their portfolios, you will probably want to assign specific partnerships. However, if students are revising or editing writing on a daily basis, it's important to let them learn to choose their own partners.

During almost every school year, my students write in a journal each day. They write best when they tell about what they know and experience. Students must show me their journal after an entry is finished. As the year progresses and students become more proficient at writing, I up the ante by having them read their journal to a friend—a sort of informal partnership. The friend must give a compliment and make a suggestion. After a while, I have these partners read aloud each other's journal entries. This is to teach the kids that their writing has an audience. They have to pay attention to what they write, how much information they include, and if their handwriting, spelling, and punctuation allow their friend to read it fluently. (Of course, if a student writes a passage that is private, it does not have to be shared with anyone.) When we get up to the journal timeline later in the year, I give children 45 minutes to do their journal and then read it to someone else. I let them choose their partner.

By that point we are doing journals twice a week and students can make productive suggestions when listening to someone else's journal.

Partnerships in Math

When I have year-long math partnerships, the children generally do most of their investigations, problem solving, and computation with their partner, about three times a week. Sometimes they do the written component together and sometimes they do their own worksheets or charts as they figure out the math procedures together. In formal math pairs, it is important that the kids are homogeneously grouped so that they can support and challenge each other without anyone taking over. It is often the case that the students can explain their mathematical thinking to each other much better than an adult can, so it's great for them to have a buddy that they are used to working with.

As with the other buddy formats for reading and writing, math buddies can be sorted informally, for specific math tasks, for short periods of time, with partners who have assorted skills. I try to use buddies a lot when I don't have a formal partnership in a curriculum area. This way, the students still have many one-on-one encounters to help them with their work.

I sometimes divide the children into groups of "double checkers" for math work. A couple of students look over each other's work to see how they did. Each gets a chance to confirm his

JOURNAL TIMELINE

✤ Think of your idea

✤ Write in your journal

✤ Read it back to yourself

✤ Edit

✤ Read your journal to a friend

✤ Hear a compliment and a suggestion

✤ Edit it again if necessary

✤ Show it to Roe

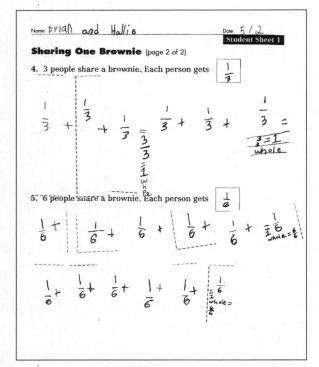

Partners help each other with a project, and do more than is asked for.

Learning From Real Life

Math Partnerships That Work

When Dylan and Hallie worked on a fraction problem, they were able to go beyond the scope of the worksheet because they knew each other so well and spurred on each other's thought processes. For this assignment, they were asked to cut each "brownie" in one way into thirds and sixths. While they were doing the thirds, they noticed that they could cut it two ways, so they figured they should do that for both thirds and sixths. They ended up cutting up each "brownie" two ways and writing the math equations on the sheet. Dylan and Hallie went beyond my expectations because they were thinking and working together.

or her thought process or to clarify his or her ideas. By learning how to double check and prove a point with someone else, the students also learn to be accountable for their independent work. If there is a discrepancy in their answers, it is their job to rethink the problem as a team.

Informal Partnerships for Varied Activities

The students in my class work in partnerships for a whole variety of activities. These pairs can happen at any time, with or without my input. As I feel it is important for the students to experience informal, free-flowing work with many children, I set up a range of opportunities for the children to be with another child. This way, the kids get to spend time with everyone in all learning venues.

One kind of varied activity that lends itself to informal partnerships happens on class trips: trips to museums, plays, dance performances, zoos, gardens, interactive places, factories and stores, local parks, etc. I let children choose their own "travelling buddy." Once we arrive at out destination, the students will generally form their own study partnerships for any activities or worksheets assigned. Sometimes, however, for certain types of group activities, I will sort them into the groups (keeping in mind which children are loud, active, or anxious, and which may tend to wander or daydream).

With opportunities to double-check, clarify, and confirm, partnerships pave the road to academic success and terrific self-esteem.

Partner Names: _____

COMMUNICATION AND ART
Look around the museum for different things that you think were used for some form of communication. Sketch (draw) what you see and write down what you and your partner think it is and/or was used for.

SKETCH	WHAT IT IS

Providing guided worksheets on trips allows partners to remain focused on the task while learning with each other.

Individual Work

Individual and group work are interdependent. Like most teachers, I want my students to achieve academic independence, meaning that each child can learn on his own. This ability to work independently is as meaningful as group negotiation and collaboration. It just so happens, though, that children become stronger individually in all areas by having so many diverse grouping experiences across the curriculum. During each and every school day, my students have tasks, projects, and worksheets that they do on their own in different subjects. They may sometimes discuss with or show their work to a partner or group, but they have tried it independently first.

Using individual work as a jumping-off point often helps group work. When students begin a project on their own, say a science research project, then come together to share ideas and present their findings in a group paper, they are getting a chance to use what they know to help the whole group. While we are focusing here on the many benefits of group work, it is important to remember that students also need solo opportunities to attempt new things and show what they know, to express themselves, to solidify knowledge and reinforce other experiences, and to have a chance to self-assess and improve their self-esteem.

CLOSING COMMENT

It is important to recognize that it is impossible to do all of these group arrangements in any given school year. Decide which variations will be right for the incoming class, which will support the children, and which will fit the components of your curriculum. You should try to have at least one stable group in each subject area, though the size of each group may differ. And remember to be flexible—I add to and modify groups and strategies throughout  the year. I plan for informal and formal groups study by study, or month by month, or week by week, or day by day, or lesson by lesson. Skillful teaching requires a lot of judgment calls.

CHAPTER THREE

WHAT'S THE PLAN?

How to Plan and Organize Groups in Your Classroom

Planning for a classroom of students revolves around a whole host
of topics. The basics have to do with curriculum mandates and
objectives, particular student needs, and the potential time
available for any given subject area. But planning also must
take into consideration how the children will perform their
tasks, and whom they'll be working with. By including the strategies for
grouping students in your overall planning work, grouping will become an
integral part of everything that is done in your classroom.

Another key issue is organization. How you organize your classroom will
affect the success of your planning and grouping. The physical space, the
rules, and the routines that get put in place at the beginning of a school year
will help allow for the greatest accomplishments of all the class members as
they grow towards autonomy and mutual reliance. And letting students
become familiar with and then take some responsibility for determining
group design and achievement supports that growth.

A thoughtful teacher is a careful planner and organizer. I am very deliberate as I plan, so that I can provide the right groupings to meet my purposes. It is also important for me to make sure that the organization of my room, and of my grouping strategies, bolsters the planning that I do. In thinking about who my students are, what my long- and short-term goals are, which groups should be stable and which should be fluid, I create an environment that nurtures group work in many and varied arrangements.

Plan for Groups

The planning process involves many steps when a teacher is preparing for a school year, week, or even day. As the teacher, you'll need to be mindful of all of the things mentioned above. In order to do that, you should consistently keep track of the subject areas to be covered, and the student needs for that particular year, with respect to curricular learning *and* grouping strategies.

For a teacher who stresses grouping, it is important to keep lists of formal groups, and to take (and hold onto) notes on how the students fare in those groups. By paying attention to the success of

Keeping notes in my plan book on grouping helps focus daily work. Groupings increase as the year goes on.

FOR WEEK 9/11/00 TO 9/15/00

THURSDAY	FRIDAY	(notes)
8:40 – JOURNAL	8:40 – JOURNAL read to "Thank You Very Much"	
9:15 – MEETING we ♥ journal / rename / park rules	9:15 – MEETING we ♥ journal / rename / words in word + list / olympics	– Start building up rug + work spot rules and routines.
9:30 – PARK	10:00 – R.W. Amelia – Tut wld rls + wlkr 2s+	– Intro some informal groupings.
10:45 – L+R		* – Remember to take notes on who works w/ who! *
11:45 – MATH guessing rule / list on board – kids represent on paper	11:40 – L+R 11:40 – MATH review – new data	– Line partners + practice
12:30 – MATH SHARE	more categories – make graph	* – I Pick potential reading partners to try out next week. *
12:40 – R. WORKSHOP (Amelia – list what she writes about with your table)	12:30 – MATHSHARE work with "Pick A Number Partner"	– TRY – RUG WORK {spots
1:20 – LIBRARY	12:50 – WORD WORK 3 let words on a list "Thank You Very Much" Partnership	LINE – WORK WITH – Read to a friend
2:05 – SNACK	1:15 – FREE TIME * discuss + rules * NO EXCLUDING	Line partner Table Group
2:15 – DESSERT read – discuss	1:55 – SNACK	Thank You Very Much Pick A Number
2:40 – QUESTION who have you been reading with? or reading to?	2:10 – ART	Turn + Talk

---

FOR WEEK 3/19/01 TO 3/23/01

THURSDAY	FRIDAY	(notes)
8:40 – READ A BOOK w/ partner	8:40 – JOURNAL a plus + a wish	
9:00 – MEETING usual / L.C.	9:15 – MEETING journal / usual / share	– gather materials for future science project.
9:30 – LEARNING CENTERS Math – create a line plot into – title labels #'s create questions w/ group handwriting – work on books writing – pick 1 story to edit + revise – review rubric comm: begin maps – look at – list / scale / key etc discuss w/ group	9:30 – R. WKSHOP lit groups – all kids in a group	– Review confusion vs. understanding to bolster Book Talks w/ r. partners
	10:20 – WORD WORK Count off pairs	– Lots of Turn + Talk!
	10:45 – L+R	* – Check on Jordan's table. Changes?? Decide??
10:45 – L+R	11:45 – PARK TRIP make a map of the park w/ 2 friends – then play	– Help from parents for Park Trip.
11:45 – L.C. (2)	1:30 – SNACK	
1:00 – DESSERT Turn + Talk	1:40 – SCIENCE PREP start research groups	– LEARNING CENTERS groups: switch Dorie + Jen!
1:30 – LIBRARY	2:10 – ART	
2:05 – SNACK		TRY Turn + Talk – bump up strats New Science Groups
2:15 – MATH 2's – count + label 3's – test prep		WORK WITH R. Partners Turn + Talk Line partner Table Group Math Buddy Short Term Writing L.C. Groups Literature Groups Informal – Park Begin Sci. Study Groups

prior experiences, a teacher can determine what would work best as a next step. It is also helpful to think about the informal groupings that have occurred, so that other formats can be tried out at different times. In this way, a teacher can use variety to add to the outcomes of grouping by planning for situations that target diverse academic and/or social objectives.

Before the Start of the School Year

As each new school year approaches, you'll need to spend a great deal of time planning the things that your students will work on. I actually try to envision the whole year so that I can begin to prepare an outline to help me with everything from the first day to the last day. My outline looks like this:

- Review things done in previous years
- Look at age/grade standards
- Go through a collection of my own worksheets
- Examine the professional books I have
- Reread helpful articles
- Study information from workshops I've attended
- Think about each topic area
- Determine the subjects or routines that will have formal groups

While I am doing all of this, I take notes to focus my work.

I write down the things that I know will be included in that year's curriculum.

For example: study mammals; write biographies; read the *My Father's Dragon* book series, investigate geometry; research rural, urban, and suburban areas.

> *To meet the standards for reading, I know that I will read the* My Father's Dragon *book series to my class. We will concentrate on comprehension strategies. I will have the students work with formal reading partners to discuss facts and inferred ideas based on our reading of the books. The students will do Turn-and-Talk projects to make text-to-text connections. After all three books are read, I will form short-term study groups to do a writing and art project that links the characters and their actions from the different books.*

I draft specific lists of the things I need to do as summer vacation draws to a close.

For example: make charts and graphs, reorganize book shelves and baskets, gather math materials, write student names on folders, type up first-day family letter.

> *The charts and graphs that I will make available for the first few weeks of school will provide opportunities for the students to work together informally. Some will be done by me, some will be completed by the students. CHARTS: Partnership Rules; Rug, Work, and Line Spots; Hundred's Board—to be filled in by math partners; Words In Words—for independent partner work. GRAPHS: How Do You Get To School?; How Many Teeth Have You Lost?; Who Has Been In Your Class Before?; What Subject Are You Good At? These will give the children a chance to work together as they fill them out, and they will provide me with specific information on some of the students.*

Before each new school year, there's a lot of organizing, outlining, listing, and labeling to be done.

I make another list of what I need to do the first few weeks of school.

Including: assess the students (see Chapter 6 for more on assessments and evaluations); hang up their first writing project; plan field trips; find out about friendships; send home class list.

> *The assessments that I do on students in reading, writing, math, and previous friendships are what inform some of the decisions that I make about how to create formal groups for students during the school year. I also carefully note which students choose to work together during informal grouping experiences so I can gauge whom they gravitate towards, and who might best support each other during academic undertakings. The assessments and grouping experiences during the first few weeks of school help set the stage for future groupings that I will try out.*

I sketch out possibilities for grouping my students.

Such as: create fixed groups for science, partnerships for math; arrange guided-reading groups by ability, writing trios by interest.

> *Over the summer, I may think I know what formal groups I want to make, but I reserve judgment until I actually meet and spend a few days with my class. Once I see the personalities, strengths, and needs of the individual students, I can then decide what kind of grouping may work best. Goals can be met by arranging to have a variety of grouping experiences throughout the year, as long as some are formal and some are informal, and are both teacher- and student-determined.*

Of course, my initial plans are just a baseline for groups. Later in this chapter, and again in Chapter 4, I will address the importance of flexibility in more depth. Flexibility is essential to planning, grouping, and teaching.

Writing a list of ideas for the school year— and for groups and partnerships—makes a good tool to refer to.

Formal literature groups forge friendships and help students focus on reading and accept accountability.

Learning From Real Life

It's All About the Kids

During most school years, I use the month of September to solidify and refine the plans that I have sketched out over the summer. One September I was trying to determine how our Reading Workshop should be arranged. I felt it was critical that year to have formal partnerships in math to nurture some needs that I had witnessed in the first week of school. Since I usually only have formal partnerships in one subject area, I decided that our reading work would involve long-term literature groups and a few short-term study groups. My planning for the rest of the month of September supported those ideas. By the beginning of October, I noticed that a handful of my students were continuing to have a hard time maintaining focus during Independent Reading time. I tried many ways to help these few children choose appropriate books, stay on task while reading, and follow up with relevant book talks. With intervention, the students were doing okay (just okay), but as soon as I went on to work with other children, those same few students lost focus. While I was doing further planning, I took some time to think carefully about how I could help these students be more independent. I realized that they needed some consistent help to sustain their reading (help that I didn't have the time for, and that I didn't think should always come from me). That kind of assistance would best come from reading partners—other children who could help the unfocused few stay engaged in a book and then have relevant book talks. I immediately planned to institute reading partnerships into our days, even though our math partnerships were in full swing. As I said, my planning usually involves only one formal partnership, but that year the needs of my students led me to plan for two formal partnerships. It worked! Those few children were able to focus better on reading because they were working with partners and had to be accountable for their reading.

As the School Year Progresses

The planning that I do during the school year is very similar to what I do over summer vacation. I review various professional sources and my own paperwork, I think about what we are studying, and I take each student's strengths and needs into consideration. I do most of my long-term planning during the summer, and again over winter break, February break, and spring break.

Whenever we start a new unit in any subject area, I sketch out the big ideas and make a list of a possible timeline for that study. If we don't already have stable groups for that subject area, I decide whether I want to form some, or if the bulk of our work will involve informal groups. I keep my long-term lists for each subject area in a folder. On the front of that folder I paperclip a large index card with the things I need to or want to do during a given week. Most of my specific planning for lessons, charts, graphs, performances, homework, and grouping arrangements is done weekly.

Weekly Planning

On Sunday nights, I write a new list in preparation for the upcoming school week. This gets done as I reflect on our previous work and think about long-term goals. The weekly list includes: the major topic areas for that week and what the children will be working on; which subjects will use groups, and how the groups will be sorted; the materials I need to gather or photocopy; paperwork that needs to be done; and phone calls that need to be made. This list helps keep me grounded as I plan. It also serves to make my time in school and at home more efficient as I try to arrange the week's activities. I also keep a plan book to write my lessons in. As I ink things into my plan book, I also decide which kinds of groups the students will be in for the different lessons and projects we'll be doing that week. The bulk of my planning gets done for the whole week as I go through this process of completing my list and plan book.

Daily Planning

At the beginning of the year, I plan one day at a time until I get to know the students well. By the end of September, our subjects and grouping routines are generally well established. For the first month, I arrange a list and a plan for each day. As the school year progresses and I've reached my weekly planning stage, I paperclip a smaller index card to the front of my folder listing all of the things that I have to get done during the very next day. I redo the daily list after school or at night. This is my chance to refine any of the plans that had been made the previous Sunday and to highlight the important things that have to be taken care of immediately. As each day of the week goes by, the success of my lessons and grouping ideas becomes clearer. I then rearrange our schedule accordingly, clarifying my weekly lists and plans with daily ones. I may be writing lists and planning a lot, but it sure feels great when I get to cross things off!

Determining Students' Group Placements

Thinking about which children will be in what groups is an extensive, often ongoing process. As the teacher, you must get to know your students individually and become familiar with what their aptitudes and weaknesses are. You must understand each area of study so that you devise the format for arranging groups that best suits the purpose of that area. You have to consider every aspect of the particular lesson you are planning so that you can decide what grouping will help students be most successful. Also to be considered are the materials required for any given activity. Reflecting on group placement is an ongoing course of action that you must rethink and rearrange constantly. Here are some of the things that I always consider:

What to think about in terms of the students:
- concept knowledge
- academic skill
- academic performance
- academic need
- friendship possibilities
- risk-taking opportunities
- emotional development
- students with behavior problems
- children who are shy or quiet
- level of engagement / enjoyment

What to think about in terms of the unit:
- subject area
- overall goals
- groupings currently in place
- prospects for success

What to think about in terms of the lesson:
- specific intent
- length of time needed
- previous and future lessons
- opportunities for challenge
- student supports

What to think about in terms of the materials:
- types of materials
- availability of materials
- how messy task may be
- ease of handling
- opportunities for sharing materials

After I contemplate most or all of these things, I am able to make good decisions about the kinds of lasting and temporary groups I will form for the school year, for a particular unit, and/or for a single lesson.

Sorting Groups: Some General Guidelines

I choose who will work together based on what the activity is. I pick students either because I need them to work with someone on their level, prefer them to be with someone who can help them, or want them to have a different experience than usual. When I place children in a formal, teacher-determined grouping, I look at my class list in advance and reflect on the study we are about to undertake. When arranging children in an informal, teacher-determined pairing, I usually do it that day, as I scan the room and think about what the students are about to do. I will make up a teacher-determined partner list the night before an activity, if I know that I need to be really specific about who works together.

Planning in Action: Groups Formed by Observation of Students' Needs

Below are some examples of how I incorporated my planning strategies to place children in appropriate grouping situations.

A Short-Term Study Group

The year my class was studying New York City as our social studies theme, our work extended into map studies of the city, our state, our country, and the earth. Then, when it came time to choose our next science subject, I noticed that the kids were becoming increasingly interested in our planet. I realized that studying the solar system would fit in with second-grade curriculum goals, and would provide some natural group work possibilities. My students would be excited by the study, and it would provide challenges and supports for different students. I set up short-term study groups, since we would work on this unit for about three weeks, with each group of three to four children focusing on a planet. And because the groups would be short term and the level of engagement would help determine the kind of work the children would do, I opted to let the students have a greater say in choosing group members.

The class discussed what our study would entail. I explained to the children that each group would study one planet, and that they would have to write a report on the planet, as well as make a model of the planet using art materials. Each child listed two planets they were interested in learning about and two children they might like to work with. It took some juggling on my part, but I was able to create short-term groups based on input from my students. I had to think about what friendships I wanted to foster and which children would need help with the research steps that this project would require.

A Cooperative Learning Group

As I've mentioned, each year my students work in literature groups so that they can read and discuss the same books. These groups are generally skill-specific, and I group the children based on reading abilities. Not long ago, I had two very verbal, bright students in my class, who both also happened to be learning disabled. As I was planning for literature groups to begin in October, I realized that I would need to think about my overall goals for the class while carefully considering the specific needs of these two students (Patty and Jack). Both were not yet fluent readers, but could understand and discuss books at deep levels.

I ended up forming long-term, heterogeneous groups for literature work so that these children—and the other students, too—could reach their potential. When selecting group members, my intent was to make sure that the students who needed reading support would be in a group with someone who was a stronger reader. I also put Patty and Jack in groups with someone they were friendly with, so they would feel comfortable.

Each group chose a book they wanted to read (from a list prepared by me), and then, group members were assigned roles. A couple of students would take turns reading, a couple of students would write notes while being read to, and a couple of students would draw illustrations of what they were hearing. I knew that Jack was a great artist, so he was one of the illustrators for his group. Patty was a quick writer (without the best spelling, but she could read her own notes), so she was one of her group's note takers. Based on student assessments and other issues that went into my planning, I had already determined that this year's literature group focus would be on comprehension. Discussion time was woven into each group session, and all the children got a chance to participate.

In my planning, I made sure to establish long-term reading partners who would meet twice a week so that Patty, Jack, and all the others could work on their strategies and skills with someone.

A Partnership

One semester, my class was going to write "How To" books. They would have to use descriptive writing to specify how to do a hobby or sport. As I was planning the unit, I thought about what grouping format I could use. I knew that one of my chief undertakings would be to help these students learn how to work with others on writing in general, which was going to be much harder than the work in the math and reading groups that they already had practice with. I resolved to create writing partnerships, so that the children would have an opportunity to work closely with someone with whom they were friendly.

The children got to pick their writing partner using a "Thank You Very Much" partnership choice (described later in this chapter). When all of the students were paired up, they got right to work. Working with someone they chose facilitated quick agreements on the "How To" topic for their partnership, and since their topic was one of mutual interest, the students were able to talk about their "How To" books in great detail. This increased the level of descriptive words they used in their pieces. The partners also managed to take turns writing and editing without much intervention from me. My planning for the skill that I wanted the students to attain and the specific tasks of the project made these partnerships the perfect grouping choice.

Willingness to Change Your Plans

Flexibility in your planning will allow you to take into account the grouping scenarios that you feel are crucial to the learning taking place in your classes. The way that you have students work with each other can change based on who they are, the ways they interact, how they progress, and what they will be doing academically as the school year continues.

Early in the year, you will have plans and ideas about the kinds of things your class will study and the groupings you will use to help students reach certain objectives. It is important to use those ideas and plans as a *guide* in your preparation, *not as a rule*. When it becomes apparent that your initial grouping plans will not fit with any current academic- or student-based requirements, you can and should make new judgment calls about grouping situations. The fluidity with which you structure and change groups based on what your students need will help them thrive. Bear in mind, though, that flexibility in group placements once the students get started on a project is another matter, and will be discussed in Chapter 4.

Organize and Establish Classroom Routines and Environment

One of the things that all teachers learn early on is that the arrangement of classroom furniture and materials helps determine the type of teaching that will take place there. Since I know that a large portion of our daily activities will involve students working together, I make sure that my room can support that need. I prefer multi-seating rectangular and round tables so that children can sit with and see each other for discussions, writing, or art projects. Even when children are working on their own, the tables in my classrooms afford them the opportunity to get help from or share ideas with others. I want to create the best academic and social possibilities, and careful room arrangements can help me do that.

Multi-seating tables work best for group work.

I try to position bookshelves around the edges of the room or at slight angles to provide as much ease of movement as possible since

Unobstructed space encourages students to get up and seek each other out for group work and to find their supplies on their own.

children will go from group to group, or from work spot to meeting area. As the students in my class become used to the supplies in our room, they have the freedom to get up and retrieve the articles they need. They can choose their own books from our library, get whatever writing materials are required, and find any other supplies that are necessary for a particular assignment. When there is a good flow of motion, the students are more willing to get up and move around when the activity warrants it.

During the first week of school, some of my mini-lessons focus on what we have in our room (I give a guided mini-tour of each area in the room), how to use classroom supplies, and when students are allowed to move about independently. By spending the time to establish the proper guidelines for how to use things and showing the children where things are, I help them be more successful during any future group work.

Later, as I introduce each new subject area to my class, we spend two or three days discussing and reviewing the methods for that subject. This can happen toward the beginning of a school year or as each new project comes up. I always start by asking students how they think our reading workshop, science work, math workshop, or art project should be run. We cover:

- ✪ What supplies can and will be used?
- ✪ How will supplies be used?
- ✪ Where should we put our things?
- ✪ Where should each child or group work?
- ✪ What are the routines for that subject?
- ✪ How will students work with, talk with, and help each other?
- ✪ What is each child's responsibility for individual or group work?
- ✪ How can work be double-checked or edited?

As a group, we ask and answer these questions so the students can take part in the decision making for our class—and to ensure that we have agreed upon rules to follow. I then tell the children my ideas and rules for certain things to finally implement the subject, activity, or project structure.

I also spend a great deal of time helping my students learn how to manage their own supplies. My students will have folders for each subject, at least two notebooks (a journal book, and a math book or social studies recording book, for instance), reading books, and other various materials. I design my classroom with different cubby spaces, folder containers, and closet areas for the students to store their things in. Exactly where and how they can store things will vary depending on the classroom we are in and the furniture and closet space available. Nevertheless, it is important for the students to learn where their things belong and to get into the habit of taking care of their books and papers. As they become better able to take care of their own things, they also learn how to take care of group supplies and materials.

There are certain organizers that I set up each school year to help the students with concentration and the flow of classroom activity. I designate the places to sit during meeting and work times. Before each independent assignment, I let the children know where in the room they can carry out the task at hand. When they are working in groups, they can choose where to sit from among the permanent configurations I've established during the first week of school. For a change of pace, I rearrange these after winter break and spring break.

Here are some things you should take into account to help with the flow of movement, work productivity, and ease of grouping possibilities:

- ✪ The table and chair arrangements
- ✪ Bookshelf and supply shelf placements
- ✪ Organization of all books and math, writing, art, and science materials
- ✪ Subjects and projects to be covered
- ✪ Storage of individual and group supplies
- ✪ Children in the class (i.e., academic and social needs)

Set Up Work and Meeting Spots

Meeting Area Spots

A large rug is a wonderful thing! I use a rug large enough for all of the children to sit around the perimeter while we have our class meetings and discussions. After I get to know the students, I take a class list and draw a map of my rug.

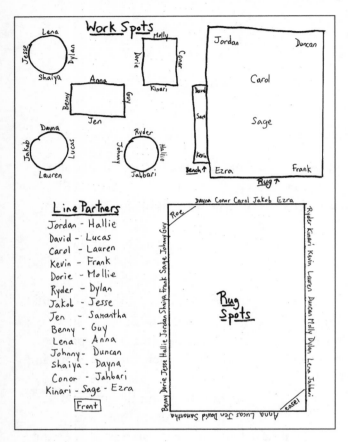

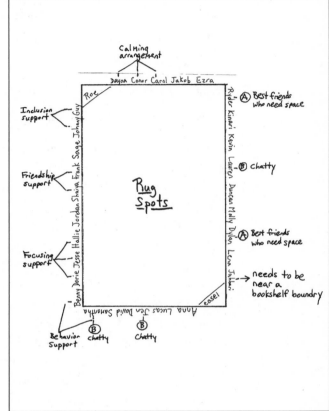

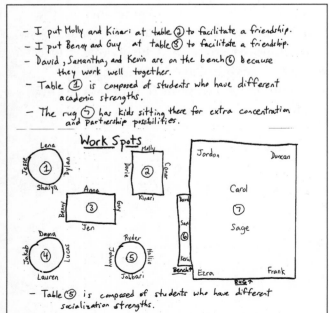

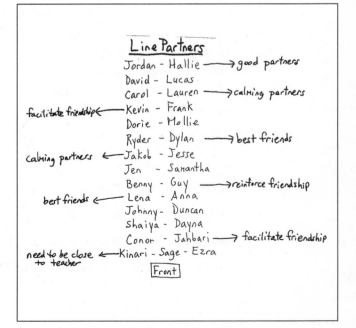

I start sorting out the students by writing down their names on my map. I arrange them around the rug, making sure to place children next to others that I think will help them concentrate. I try not to put them next to their best friends. The teacher shouldn't be the only center of attention during class meetings, so I place children along the edges of the rug during discussion times. This way they can look at each other and listen intently to whoever is talking. First, I mark students who are distractible on the map, making sure to spread them out. Then I write in the names of children who focus well near those who need more assistance. I position some of the students who have good self-control near bookshelves, since others might not be able to pay attention there. My rug spots also end up being close to a boy-girl pattern, which further assists me in making sure the children aren't sitting right next to someone they might be prone to chat with.

Comfortable Rug Spots

Our classroom rug is central to many of the things that we do as a whole class. Meeting-area spots help us have whole-group discussions and keep the students focused on each other. This same rug (or a taped-off floor area if a teacher doesn't have access to a rug) functions another way when I ask the students to "sit in a comfortable spot."

Whenever I read aloud, go over a poem, diagram or graph, write on the chalkboard or chart paper, or use the overhead projector, I tell the students to "get in a comfortable spot." This is the signal to congregate close to me so that they can focus on what we are doing. The students' attention is now on the task at hand—and the children are given a chance to sit next to students they are developing a relationship with. They often choose to sit near those students that they are currently in a group with or working on a project with. The children know that "once they choose a spot, they stay there" (an oft-repeated classroom phrase that reminds them not to scoot around). There are a few students who gravitate towards the back because they have a hard time concentrating, so I may tell two or three particular students that they have to sit near me. If I am reading from chapter books without illustrations, the children may lie down if they'd like, so that they can "make pictures in their minds."

Work Spots

Since the tables and chairs in my room are already organized to allow for ease of movement, I assign students spots at tables for their independent work times. I have found that it is advantageous to do this early in the year so that they can really concentrate while they are doing projects or worksheets on their own. As with the "rug spots," I start figuring out these arrangements by drawing a map of the tables in my room and writing down names based on where I think children should sit. And again, I think about who gets distracted and who is distracting, but for work spots I do focus more on facilitating friendships as well. While I often put really close friends at different tables so that they can get used to working with other students, I will group the students so that there is someone that each child can feel at ease with at their table. I also contemplate each student's academic and social skills because I want someone at each table who can read well, write efficiently and/or explain things easily. I also place at least two children with similar abilities at each table so they can feel that they have peers on their level to sit with. These students are usually already in an established homogeneous partnership, such as writing partners. With careful planning, each table becomes a mini cooperative-learning group.

Line Partners

One of the things I start telling the children on the first day of school is that we have to pay attention to safety, learning, and fun. Since we walk all over the school, take a class trip each month, and sometimes go to local stores or parks, I need to know that the students can line up and travel in a secure and calm manner. I select line partners so that I know we can accomplish those two things. I don't want the children to disturb other classes when we are navigating our hallways nor to lose focus when we are out of the school building. And there may be unpredictable situations when we go on excursions, so I must make sure that the children can see and hear me. In a sense, line partners is another very important type of grouping. I pick line partners based on the same theories of facilitating concentration, fostering new associations, and ensuring ease of movement that I use for rug and table spots. I put more self-reliant students towards the back of the line, and those I'll need to monitor closest to me. I sometimes allow students to pick their line partners, but I always pick the partners' position in the line.

As I mentioned earlier, I determine the formal work areas, rug spots, and line spots in September and January. In April, when we switch for our third spot rotation, I let the children choose whom they will sit next to on the rug and at work spots. By this point in the year, the students know each other well and have had a good deal of practice in choosing partners and groups and following classroom procedures and rules. They now can make good choices about whom to work with and whom they may need a break from.

Friendships

As I've stated, I believe that it is important to plan groups that will foster friendships. There are some students who will come to your class with friends from previous school years. There are others who make friends easily and find ways to be with different children. There are also some children who don't have any friends from prior classes, who don't make friends easily, who have a hard time keeping friends, or are new to the school and neighborhood. One of the best ways you'll find to help spark a friendship is putting two children together in a few areas. Sit them at the same table (or desk cluster), make them line partners, put them in each other's learning center groups, and in other informal partnerships as well. If you see that things

Learning From Real Life

Good Planning Lasts a Long Time

Recently I bumped into a former student. Evan, who is now in high school, entered my class as a second grader new to the school. He was having a hard time with the transition to a new city and a new learning environment. The first thing I recognized was that he needed an anchor to help him settle in. I thought that Evan's class time and lunch/recess would be made easier if he had a friend. I knew that Jesse would be a perfect choice. I made them line partners, put them in the same literature group, and spoke to both of their families about setting up play-dates. Before I knew it, they were inseparable. When summer vacation arrived, I remember thinking that Evan's year was successful because he'd had someone to share it with. When I saw Evan, one of the first things he said to me was, "Jesse and I picked the same high school." Putting these children in a few grouping situations had blossomed into something so much more than even I could have imagined. Ten years later they were still inseparable!

Investigate, Then Plan

One year, I had three students in my class who seemed to get into arguments and disagreements during independent activities, free time, and at recess. Rachel, Alex, and Loretta were all sweet, calm children. Yet often I would hear snippets about the problems they were having during the school day. Rachel's mom even came to the school to talk to me about how upset Rachel was when she came home from school on most days. I planned to separate the children during group activities to try to alleviate the problems. After a couple of weeks, I noticed that they were still having disagreements. I decided that it was time to investigate the situation. What I found out is that Rachel and Alex were best friends in preschool, but were in different kindergarten classes and didn't really see each other much that year. In kindergarten, Rachel and Loretta became best friends and even spent time together during the summer vacation before first grade. When all three children got to my class, Alex was jealous of the friendship that Rachel and Loretta had developed. During different class projects and at recess, Alex and Loretta were fighting for Rachel's attention. Rachel was torn between her friends, and didn't know how to choose between them without hurting someone's feelings.

After I had examined their history, I realized what I had to do. Some children don't know how to play with more than one child at a time, and find it hard to share a friend. I used my planning time and skills to find ways to bring Alex and Loretta together so that they could develop a friendship. I put them both in the same literature group since they had similar skills, and I assigned them to be permanent math partners. As time went on and the girls got to know each other better, I put all three into a study group to research some leaves we had collected. Alex and Loretta got to know and like each other, and Alex, Loretta, and Rachel got to practice how to interact in a group of three. While some envy did persist for a few weeks, the three students eventually found a way to get along. The icing on the cake for me was on a day when I was picking the class up from recess and I heard Loretta say, "The three Musketeers are getting on line!"

are going well between the two students, speak with them and their families about the possibility of setting up play-dates.

Activities for Helping Students Form Groups

Teachers will spend a great deal of time arranging many grouping situations for their students, all the while recognizing that the point of these groups is to help the students grow towards independence. One of the best ways you can help students achieve this is to give them many opportunities to take part in the decision-making process for certain grouping circumstances.

Some groups will function better because the children get to choose their co-workers. At other times, it simply isn't necessary for you to be in control of who works together. Moreover, by letting the children choose various group members, you get to see how well the students are forming new friendships and making decisions about which students they can best work with for certain subject areas.

By discussing the many grouping situations together with your class, you are supporting the development of skills and strategies with respect to the reasons for working with others and making good partner/group choices. As I try to infuse my students with a sense of independence, I often let them form their own groups or partnerships, placing absolutely no restrictions on those choices, other than the rules my students learn during the modeling of other group choice events. But there are quite a few "methods" for choosing partners and groups. Here are the most successful methods (which I've invented or learned from other teachers) that fit a variety of purposes.

Thank-You-Very-Much Partnership

The children get to choose their partners. If one student is chosen before he or she had a chance to pick a partner, that student must say "thank you very much" and join the student who made the choice. The teacher calls on one child, who then walks over to the student he or she wants to work with. This system allows those children without a good friend to have a chance to select someone they will feel comfortable with. It's a good idea to discuss this kind of partnership early on in the year. Talk about the fact that kids can easily become disappointed or sad, but that the class will choose partners a lot, so they will get to work with various children many, many times. The students are quick to understand that they'll have some formal, teacher-determined, long-term partnerships, but that they'll also get to spend a lot of short-term time with different children during math investigations, science mini-units, and many other lessons. You may also want to role play choosing partners, so the students know the process and the possibilities for success. As part of that role play, you can suggest things like, "Choose someone you haven't spent a lot of time with," or "Pick a person you want to get to know," or "Select a boy if you're a girl and a girl if you're a boy."

Thank-You-Very-Much partnerships often bring about valuable and unexpected results.

Pick a Number

We sometimes pull numbers out of a bag to form groups. For my class of 28 students, if I want pairs of children to work together, I will put two sets of the numbers 1 to 14 in a bag (for groups of three, I'll use three sets of the numbers 1 to 10) and have the kids pick out a number. The children will work together with the other person who has the same number. I like to use the Pick-a-Number process for small task groups in writing, reading, or for word study. The children can support each other with their different strengths, and when they randomly choose numbers, they often end up making great heterogeneous groups. This procedure also works well for informal, short-term groups.

Pick a Card

The playing cards that we use for some math activities can also become a quick and easy tool for sorting students into groups. Our "make 10" decks already have the face cards removed, and if I intend for the children to work in fours, I can simply take out the 8s and 9s, and shuffle the remaining cards. Each student then picks a card, and all the 1s work together, all the 2s, etc. The children get very excited when we do Pick a Number or Pick a Card because the choices are random. Since Pick a Card makes groups of four, it works well for projects and art groups, and even for a literature or writing-genre study. We do have a class discussion (and reminders) about appropriate behavior: students cannot make a face or say anything unkind if someone they are not fond of ends up in their group.

Count Off

After calling the students together, I may walk around the perimeter of the rug and "count off" children to form groups. I decide how many students will be in each group and then count out that number, tapping the students as I do. Just as in Pick A Card, all the 1s work with each other, all the 2s, etc. Depending on the number of students and the size of the groups, a couple of groups may contain one student more or less than the others. I sometimes use Count Off to form short-term learning centers groups, social studies mini-units, or math investigations.

Turn and Talk

When I ask the class a question or we are having a group discussion, it is not always possible for everyone to have a turn. Even after a mini-lesson, when students are given individual or group work time to share what they've done, there may be time constraints that keep everyone from participating, or it just might be too hard for the kids to sit and listen to each and every child. However, there are definite occasions when I want *all* of the children to be able to express themselves. I discovered that a fun and manageable solution to this problem was to allow the students to talk to one or two other people near them, then come back together as a group. I'll say, "Turn and talk to someone near you. Make sure everyone is involved in a conversation." I give the groups a two-minute warning to finish the conversation. Then I turn on the lights as a signal to get back to the whole-class meeting. When we reassemble, four or five kids may end up sharing what they were thinking with the whole group, but each child has already had a chance to talk.

Turn and Talk is also a wonderful strategy for practicing students' "attending" skills. I may pose a question for partners to discuss, students may generate a question for their partner to answer, or partners give each other

Groupings like Turn and Talk give every single child a chance to speak and listen.

information on a book or an experience. When we return to the whole group, the children must retell what their partner said. Verbal communication is a two-way process, so the children need to practice listening as much as they need to practice speaking. These listening and retelling drills are perfect for reminding students to attend to each other's words carefully.

Group Work in Action

GETTING STUDENTS STARTED BY GETTING INVOLVED

When my class was doing a Turn and Talk about snow, (we were about to study snow for a weather unit), one student, Sandy, approached me.

Sandy: *Roe, I have nobody to talk to.*

Roe: *Why don't you talk with Tom and Raisa? They're sitting right near where you were before.*

Sandy: *I want my own partner; they already have each other.*

All of the kids had a pair and three kids were absent so we had an odd number in the room that day. I didn't want to make Sandy uncomfortable by plopping her in a group, so I sat down with her, right near Tom and Raisa.

Roe: *What do you know about snow?*

Sandy: *Well, it's from rain, and if it's cold it comes down as snow, and if I can, I lick it right out of the air.*

Roe: *You're kidding me? What's it like?*

By this point Tom and Raisa were watching us talk.

Sandy: *One time a snowflake landed on my tongue, and it didn't melt, so my sister said it looked like I had a crystal in my mouth.*

Roe: *A crystal! Why did she say that?*

Raisa: *Because snowflakes are shaped like crystals.*

Tom: *They all have different shapes.*

Sandy: *And I know that two are never the same.*

Tom: *I got snow flying in my window one day when I left it open.*

Roe: *You three know a lot about snow. Keep talking while I get some things we'll need after Turn and Talk.*

TEACHER'S TAKE: The teacher can be a big draw sometimes. By starting a conversation with Sandy, I was able to intrigue the children near us, get them involved in the exchange, and then move on. Sandy took a risk by coming to me for help, but was too shy to venture into a dialogue that was already taking place between Tom and Raisa. My actions got Sandy into their group without any embarrassment, and they all continued to talk exuberantly.

Think-Pair-Share

Think-Pair-Share is very similar to Turn and Talk. Two or three kids get together to discuss a topic or figure something out, then the whole class convenes to hear what the pairs did. The difference with this arrangement is that the teacher plays more of a role in choosing the pairs, and each of the pairs gets a turn to relate what was discussed when the class comes back together. Since each partner already had a chance to talk with the other, only one tells the whole class what they talked about. This way, each child's ideas, understanding, remarks, or opinions can be presented to the whole class without a lengthy (or tedious) meeting. This works well for many projects, especially those involving research or an investigation.

Letters, Colors, and Numbers

If my class is doing a single-lesson or quick activity that involves working with a few children, and I want to infuse a little fun in forming groups, I will use letters, colors, or numbers. It's a fast, fun, and active way to create random groups and get started on the activity. I might say "Everyone whose name starts with the letters A, B, C, D, or E is in one group; F, G, H, I J, K, or L is in another group," and so on. I can also sort by colors: "Anyone wearing red come and learn this math game, everyone wearing blue come and learn this math game, everyone wearing brown...," and so on. On other occasions I may sort the students by numbers: "All students with 3 or 4 letters in your first name work here, and all children with 5 or 6 letters work here." Obviously, each of these formats may require a little tweaking based on the configurations of class initials, clothing colors, or number of letters in a name. However, this is something active that the children enjoy—and that requires them to start thinking even before an activity begins.

Impromptu Groups

Believe it or not, sometimes I just tell the kids to have a conversation with or play with others, and there are *no* follow-up discussions. Students should know that not all grouping or partnership activities must be determined by me or by any specific strategy. We all have people we'd like to spend time with, and projects we'd like to delve into with someone in particular. Children form friendships naturally and become involved with each other when they have similar interests. I use grouping strategies to help improve and increase my students' interactions and socializations, but I want them to have some autonomy and decision-making possibilities—and I want them to have a chance to put these developing skills to use *naturally*. By allowing them to make some of their own choices, I'm also giving the children a chance to practice and use all of the skills that our grouping situations are providing them with.

In my class, I schedule free time once or twice a week for 30-40 minutes. Since it is *free* time, the children can play with anyone and use any of the materials we have in class. The only restrictions I place on how the student's play are that: 1) if someone takes the risk of trying to join a group, they cannot be excluded; and 2) if a student sees someone playing alone, the student should invite that child to join their group. (And of course, all "clean up" procedures apply.) We also go to a local park about once a month, and I don't feel that I should control grouping for that situation; the children play with whomever they like. Free time and park trips are privileges that the class earns based on their dedicated work and appropriate behavior. I think that it is crucial for young learners that some of their interactions in class be purely social, purely enjoyable, and based mostly on private decisions.

CLOSING COMMENT

To develop all of the skills and strategies necessary in my classroom, I make sure to incorporate a variety of grouping activities to bolster any and all academics, while staying true to the needs of social and emotional growth. This can only happen when I set up certain structures that will support group work, and when I devote considerable time and effort to plan out the grouping situations. I try to use all of the procedures and techniques listed in this chapter to help my students reach those goals that I propose for them, and those that they themselves decide are necessary.

Teaching children how to collaborate and expand their academic and social skills requires careful planning and organizing. Setting up an environment that fosters emotional growth does, too. As you take the time to plan for good scholastic endeavors, be aware of the holistic needs of children. And remember, the ways in which a teacher introduces and follows through on classroom practices for grouping will have a great impact.

CHAPTER FOUR

HOW ARE YOU MANAGING?

Keeping Your Groups Running Well and Moving Students When Necessary

I believe that one of my primary duties as a teacher is to give students the opportunities to work both independently and with others—and to do so in positive ways. In order to do this, we need to be mindful of some basic elements as we place children in groups, and as we mediate different grouping formations to ensure that they remain successful. Classroom management is a major factor in helping children meet their potential, and this remains true for a teacher who utilizes grouping as a basis for student achievement. The specific rules and routines teachers implement all work toward regulating individual and group interactions. Students need consistency in class management so that they know what to do. They also need assistance with lessons and activities during transitions, when difficult grouping situations need to be rearranged.

When planning, think about all of the things covered in Chapters 2 and 3 as you decide how to form associations. You'll need to consider whether they are random or teacher- or student-determined groupings; heterogeneous or homogeneous; long-term or short-term; and you'll need to think about what student personalities and backgrounds, special needs and particular strengths come into play. Once your groups are in place, the next crucial steps are those that involve figuring out what is working and what needs modification.

Occasionally, students may end up in groups that are too easy or too challenging for them, or they may outgrow a grouping academically or socially. In my experience, there have been instances when I make mistakes or misjudge a child's placement. As you monitor the different group work that your class does, be sure to stay flexible about moving children around so that they continue to prosper. Reflect on the management techniques you have in place, and determine if you need to reinforce these, or if it is actually time to move some students around. By taking all of these factors into account as you make and adjust groupings, you will better maintain a holistic approach to teaching and learning.

Some Basics in Classroom Group Management

In any classroom, the ways in which a teacher establishes rules and routines influences the kind of work students are able to accomplish. Teachers should be explicit, right from the start, about *what* students can and should do, and *when* they can and should do those things. From the very first day of school, I have the children enter into whole-class discussions about the roles that we all need to assume in order to make our time together as productive and enjoyable as it can be. By involving the students in our classroom regulation decisions, I am enabling them to feel that we are all one community, responsible for and to each other, as we maneuver through our school year.

In fact, I begin one of our very first whole-class meetings by reminding the children that

Consistent rules, routines, and roles help make class time as productive and enjoyable as possible.

they have all been in other classes (earlier grades) before and asking them to think about rules that they used in those classes. I pose two very specific questions:

✤ What rules do we need for safety, learning, and fun?

✤ Why do we need to have those rules?

It is definitely a good idea to phrase the questions so that children think about *what* they should do, and *why* they should do those things. Otherwise, you'll get a list with lot of "NO" ideas: *no calling out, no pushing, no being silly, no teasing*, etc. This kind of a discussion does not lead to getting at acceptable behavior and work habits, and what you want to establish is how we all can and should interact with each other. Plus, when you frame the questions in a positive way, you are sending the message that children *can and do know what is expected* of them.

A few years ago my students and I made a list of rules that we repeated during some morning meetings all year long. We hung it up in the classroom, and I have reused the same list in other school years after initial discussions with the class. While the rules are general in nature, they are easily applied to any grouping or partnership situation. Whatever rules get established during the first few days of school are the ones that we refer to all year long.

Once we start instituting long-term and short-term groups, our conversations become more specific about how these groups and partnerships can work. I create rubrics with my class to delineate ways to be a successful member of a group, listing objectives, levels of achievement, and the rules for appropriate participation in a specific group or activity. In our discussions, we detail what kinds of behaviors are essential, and what behaviors don't meet good partnership/group goals for different group formats and subject areas. I then create a sign and post it in the classroom for future reference.

CLASSROOM RULES
(To promote safety, learning, and fun!)

Always try to do your best work

Be fair and polite to others

Listen while someone is speaking

Respect books, materials, and each other

Put things in proper places

Only touch people in gentle ways

Try to help or be helped when needed

Treat and speak to others as you would want to be treated

Be responsible, concentrate, cooperate, and...

SMILE!

WAYS TO WORK WITH A PARTNER

GREAT PARTNER!	KEEP TRYING!
Works together	Works alone
Looks at partner	Looks around
Listens	Gets distracted
Speaks clearly	Mumbles
Takes turns	Takes over
Focuses on partner	Moves near a friend
Asks for explanations	Lets unknown information slide by
I Messages	You Messages
Put Ups	Put Downs

Posting behavior guidelines enables students to self-monitor to keep things running smoothly.

Managing Groups and Partnerships

Whenever you start a new grouping or partnership in class, your first discussion should be about rules. Together with your students, delineate the guidelines for work and the behavior expectations that pertain to the specific assignment. Involve the children in a constructive way by asking them what they think will work, and then tell them the things you know will be helpful. It is also beneficial to review general class and partner rules. These discussions can take place as a whole class or sometimes with the particular group. (See *Modeling Group Behavior for Students* in Chapter 5.)

As you circulate from group to group, look for signs that tell you if a child is having a problem. Check to see if something is too hard or too easy for students, and look for appropriate participation and turn taking. You should also assess social interactions. If you notice a problem in any of these areas, quickly think about how the snag can best be untangled. Sometimes students will tell you when they or others are experiencing difficulties.

When a problem arises, the first step is to let the students in a group or partnership attempt to work it out, independently or with teacher-guided discussions. Talk with the students about the specifics and refer to the rules to see if that will help. If this does not resolve the problem or difficulty, then you must consider regrouping and act swiftly in carrying this out. Never let a problem fester or grow out of control.

Managing Individual Students

When a child is having difficulty in a group, you may not want to involve the whole group in the discussion. It is often best to ask the child to meet with you privately, so that you can talk about what's going on. When this happens, it is a chance for you to see more clearly if the problem is academic or social. The primary problems usually have to do with work being too challenging or simple (academics), or involve personality clashes with other group members (social). Students don't always want to share that information in front of others.

I like to try to brainstorm ideas with the student about how he or she could better maintain membership in the group. Sometimes a child needs more kindness and support from the group members, and sometimes he or she may need a bit more teacher assistance. When the group hasn't been able to work out a problem together, I always give the individual students a chance to work it out their own. However, if discussions, teacher support, and teacher interventions don't work, then I know it is time to change groupings or partnerships.

Reaching Behavioral Potential

As any teacher knows, student behavior varies quite dramatically. Each child's background, personality, and prior experiences affect the way they interact in a classroom. While we set up whole-class behavioral expectations together, some students have a hard time living up to those expectations. And though it is important for teachers (and fellow students) to remain consistent regarding the expectations, the fact is that some students need help behaviorally. Children may call out, try to do other things besides the given activity, leave a group, hurt someone, or just generally fool around.

In addition to all of the discussions and reminders about classroom rules and good work behavior, I institute certain structures in my class to help keep children focused. I've already pointed out the possibility of choosing group members as a way to help some students reach and maintain good conduct; this is perhaps the best and most reliable method. However, if I am lucky enough to have a student teacher or paraprofessional, I ask that adult to shadow a child who is having difficulty and provide necessary assistance. When that doesn't work, I turn to some other techniques that reward "good work" and penalize students who are not doing their best work or are holding up the progress of a group.

Rewards

I strive to use a lot of positive reinforcement in class. I praise children for their academic and social accomplishments—and make sure that these comments are given for real progress, so as not to overuse praise. I teach the children to compliment each other more often as well. My class learns that a PUT UP is the opposite of a PUT DOWN. The students quickly discover that they have the power to help each other out just by the manner in which they talk to one another. I also give the children stickers for good work. They love to get and collect these stickers, sometimes putting them on their work or on the cover of a notebook.

During group or partnership situations, good behavior is rewarded by the outcome of the groups' work. The children who finish their responsibilities can have free time while the rest of the class is still working. Students enjoy helping a teacher, so many of the tasks I ask the children to do with or for me are based on their behavior. If I recognize that children are trying to do their best, they can help me sort papers, go on errands, organize materials, lead the line, give out snack, and many other things of that nature. Some children also like to stay in class during recess. I will let children who have reached a behavioral goal pick a friend to stay in with them, and they can play or draw.

Penalties

Sometimes it becomes necessary to censure students when they are behaving improperly and other tactics have not aided them in following through on their responsibilities. I have applied many behavior management strategies over the years that have worked. It is easy to add extra recess, free time periods, trips to the yard and park, and art projects to promote good behavior. Likewise, I can decrease these experiences or take them away when the majority of children are not responding to general class rules.

When individual children are behaving poorly in a group, I will first give them warnings, and then reduce or suspend one of the above-mentioned privileges. At the very beginning of the year, I inform students that they if they get three verbal warnings in any given day, they will get "time out" and have five minutes deducted from the next privilege activity. If a child gets time out a lot, I will contact the family so that we can all discuss what's going on. Sometimes I will remove a child from a group to think about, discuss with me, and/or write about what he or she is doing wrong and what can be done to improve the behavior.

Switching a child's group placement or partnership is sometimes a punishment in itself. When students are having a hard time concentrating, taking measures that remind them about the fact that they really do like their group members is sometimes enough to get them to work harder. On that rare occasion when a child persists in disrupting the group and the whole class, I make arrangements with other teachers to allow my students to work in their rooms. I may send my student along with a letter like this:

Dear _____,

I had to leave my group and classroom.

May I stay in your class and work quietly for 10 minutes?

I need to finish my work.

I also need to observe and think about appropriate behavior, good work habits, and self-control.

Thank You, _____

Helping Students Remain On Task

It is the teacher's responsibility to circulate through the classroom to make sure that everyone is on task. Losing focus can result from a student's lack of confidence, the difficulty of a specific task, or behavioral issues. Students with difficult behavior are often those who just don't feel that they can accomplish certain things. Teachers can use adult guidance, partner assistance, reminders, and positive reinforcement to try to help children sustain their concentration and complete their work.

There are times when I try to have the whole class working in teams, and a couple of children just can't seem to handle it. I want to give them the possibility to do the best they can, so occasionally I will let a couple of kids work alone while the rest of the class works in groups. And again, if some pairings are just not working out, it becomes necessary to allow some students to perform the assignment individually. There are other occasions when I specifically arrange activities that allow my students to work on their own or with a partner. At these times, I let them decide what they would be most comfortable with. I am most likely to present students with this option when we are doing research, certain math investigations, or writing projects.

I will sometimes allow for modifications in expectations for certain students, too. I may expect most students to write three pages for a given assignment, but will let someone with concentration problems write two pages. While all of the students have to read four chapter books in a month, I may require one student to read only two. And again, if all of the children in a group are supposed to do research, a child who could not accomplish this would take on a different role, such as the note taker or project illustrator. These kinds of modifications can also help students remain on task.

I have created checklists to help children

Students having trouble with a project can remain involved as note-takers or illustrators.

get through all of the day's activities. It is sometimes useful to break down goals into small, attainable steps. By creating checklists, tailored to different students and to that year's subjects, I can help children work towards their goals slowly. This tool helps keep them focused and, at the end of the day, they may get a reward or a nice note for their families to read.

BEHAVIOR AND WORK CHECKLIST					
	Monday	Tuesday	Wednesday	Thursday	Friday
Morning Work					
Meeting					
Reading Partner					
Math Team					
Lunch					
Recess					
Writing Group					
Project Work					
Line Up					
Other					

When Should You Switch a Child's Placement?

When the students' own efforts or your intervention (all the reminders, reinforcements, rewards, and penalties) still cannot resolve a problem, then it's time for you to make a switch. Although you have carefully considered the groupings before they are formed, and sometimes the children have actually chosen their group members, remember that *all groupings are adaptable*. It is good for the students to see that we can make changes when things are not working out, and to learn that there are many ways to make a situation beneficial for everyone involved.

For the most part, it is easy to recognize the need for an academic change in homogeneous groups and partnerships. With such groups, you can tell when a child needs more support or challenges. A change will benefit a child who is not achieving success, and this change can happen without disrupting other groups. Since heterogeneous groupings allow all of the children to participate in different ways, you usually only have to rearrange certain students when a behavior or personality problem occurs. In general, if a group seems to be working out, let it run its course (and remember, sometimes "success" is different from the goal you had in mind for the group). If it isn't working, consider making a change.

When It Works; When It Doesn't

The grouping arrangements that get made during the course of a year fall into many categories. Beyond the variety of groupings, there are also a variety of successes. Groups work when kids can focus, when they get along, and when good work and discussion occurs. I want my students to take more responsibility for negotiation and accept more accountability as the months pass, and therefore I make sure to give them plenty of opportunities to be with various children. Pairings work when the students get to do some things independently. They will also work when the students and teacher have set intervention strategies in place by first discussing what to do if a problem arises. Changes only make sense when you give the children a chance to work it out on their own before you step in.

The structure and strategies that you weave throughout a school year allow the students to make general groupings successful. There may be obstacles for a couple of children, but that very rarely affects the entire class. Collections of students don't work when a teacher hasn't thought through the assignment carefully enough. A teacher needs to be very deliberate about planning to make sure that a project is good for more than one child to do, and that it is not too easy or hard. Over the years, I have occasionally made some wrong decisions about what kinds of groups to use for an activity. Groups usually don't work if I haven't outlined the assignment or grouping carefully enough. It is also crucial that I let all of the students know that they can help to make a grouping work. I try to empower them so that the onus doesn't only fall on me.

Particular Situations That Require a Switch

Work Spots

My students do about half of their daily activities sitting at their work spots. I try to arrange it so that they are at a table with children they can talk to, but who will not distract them from their work. Generally, only two things could happen that would lead me to change a child's work spot. Either someone can't focus on his work because he is too busy gabbing, or a child is upset because she is having disagreements with another student. Before I can make a change, I need to review where everyone else is sitting, so that as I make a switch, I maintain the integrity of the other work tables.

Rug Spots

We also spend a lot of time meeting and sharing ideas on our rug. While the kids are sitting around the borders, I keep my eyes open for any signs of difficulty. There are a few basic things that might prompt me to move a child from his or her rug spot. When I have a student who is suddenly having a hard time focusing or is calling out often, I end up putting that child near my seat. More often, however, a gentle touch on the shoulder or a glance from me will help the students remain engaged. If a student is spending a lot of time chatting with her neighbor, I

Learning From Real Life

Asking the Right Questions

*J*ack was one of those students who are puzzling to a teacher. He had a lot of abilities in many areas. One of his main strengths was speaking. When I read a part of a book with him and talked to him about it, he did just fine. He decoded the words in the story well and had a really good grasp of what was going on. This assessment led me to put him a literature group that was about to start the very book he had read an excerpt from with me. I worked with that group, and while Jack's reading was a bit slow, he managed to sound out the words. He also did a fabulous job of participating in our discussions. When it came time for a new book, I noticed that Jack continued to decipher the words well, but was unable to join in our conversations. I pulled him aside to have a chat. What I discovered was that his father had read the previous book to him at home, so he had had a lot of opportunities to talk about it. I realized that while he was able to read well, his comprehension skills were at a very different level from the rest of the group's. I made the mistake of not asking him if he had ever heard the first book before. Now I make sure to always ask that question whenever I read with a student. This way I can monitor their decoding and comprehension and place them in the right reading arrangement.

FACILITATING CHANGE

Johnny was at a table with a few talkative students. He really tried to get them to stop talking so he could focus on his own work. Finally, he approached me.

Johnny: *Roe, I keep asking those kids to stop talking, but they won't.*

Roe: *What kinds of things have you said?*

Johnny: *I told them that they were distracting me and that it was a quiet work time. This happens every day!*

Roe: *Let me have a try.*

I sat down at the table and had a talk with the whole group. A few days later, Johnny came back to me.

Johnny: *It's still happening. I just can't do my work.*

Roe: *Okay, I'll make a change.*

I surveyed the room to figure out which student I could switch with Johnny.

Roe: *Dylan, I'd like to move your spot to Johnny's seat.*

Dylan: *Why?*

Roe: *Johnny is having a hard time concentrating. You've done nothing wrong, but I think you may be able to focus at that table and he can't.*

Dylan: *Okay, I'll give it a try.*

TEACHER'S TAKE: I needed to let Dylan know that this change was not about him. I also had another talk with Johnny's original table because they did need to start concentrating—with or without Johnny sitting there. As it turned out, the move was good for Johnny and fine for Dylan. Dylan had a higher tolerance for a little noise, and Johnny now sat at a table that was quieter.

will give her a few chances to stop, then I will move her. If a child can't keep his hands off of books or materials on a bookshelf, I will put him in a rug spot that is clear of potential distractions. There have also been occasions when two children stop getting along. One may start poking at or teasing another. Sometimes I try to help them work through it, and sometimes it seems better to head off any further problems by making a substitution.

Important ideas are shared on our rug; it's key not to let students get distracted by other things.

Long-Term Partnerships and Groups

As students work together in their long-term partnerships or groups, I walk around the room to see how they are progressing and assist them with the assignments if necessary. If I notice that a child is having a hard time academically, initially I try to let a partner or other group members help out. If the problem persists, I need to take action myself. This tends to be the case only if the child's ability level does not allow him or her to participate in the group activity and the other students' skills are too different to support his or her needs. In any event, when this occurs, I switch the struggling child into a different partnership or group. Even though I want students to help each other, I do not want to place too much responsibility on any one child or group. An association has to be mutually beneficial.

Short-Term Groups

Randomly-selected and short-term associations generally fare better than long-term partnerships because students know that they don't have to be together for the whole year, and because skill level is usually not a factor. I may have to move children around initially, but that doesn't happen too often. More typically, I will need to move a whole partnership or group to a different place in the room. For instance, a collection of kids may sit near their friend's group and then not focus on the work their own group is doing. I will simply let the students know that they need to take their work to another area of the classroom. These kinds of switches are easy to make and allow the groups to continue their good work.

Learning From Real Life

Together—Sometimes

When Erik was in my class, he had a good relationship with Max. They played together at recess, were in the same reading group, and had some play-dates at home. I decided to make permanent math partnerships that year. I wanted the partners to have similar skills, and because Erik and Max did, I thought it would be nice to put them together. After a few math games and lessons, Erik started coming over to me to complain about Max. Max was taking over the projects. I sat the boys down to talk about it a few times. It turned out that Max thought his mathematical thinking was superior to Erik's. Since Erik was not a big risk taker, he just shut down. They both tried to make the partnership work, but Max kept doing most of the work and Erik kept letting him. Erik would come to talk to me when no one else was around because he was losing confidence and getting frustrated. After some careful consideration, I decided to switch their partnership so that I could help preserve their friendship.

Academic Needs

It is not uncommon for a child to make sudden dramatic strides academically. If such a child is in a group that requires all students to be on or about the same level, I will need to move him or her into a new group. Planning and grouping strategies must allow for scholastic growth spurts. If I have initially made an error with a child's year-long placement—for instance, placing her in a literature group or math partnership that is too hard or easy—I'll keep this child with her group until the current book or project is completed, monitoring the situation closely. Then I'll switch her into a more appropriate group.

Having grouped children in a variety of ways, I've noticed that there are occasions when certain children flourish together. Those same children, on the other hand, will experience times and circumstances when they don't work well together. Whether students become good academic work partners or develop a pleasant social friendships, it is not always prudent to have the same children working together all of the time. It is a teacher's job to figure out not only which students can work together, either for academic or social growth, but how often they should work together.

How to Resolve Special Problems

All children have distinct personalities, academic skills, and behavior patterns. Those are the things that make each class a joy. The differences we all have allow us to learn from each other and enrich the interactions we experience each school day. I love the way that the students inspire each other, help each other, and take risks because of what they notice from every member of our class.

While all children function in a classroom in different ways, there are certain extreme behaviors, learning needs, and student background experiences that exceed the typical variations in and among students. There are a variety of problems that can affect the proper functioning of a group or partnership. Some of these problems have been detailed throughout this chapter, but there are a couple of specific ones I want to cover here.

Social Problems in Groups

Sometimes a child experiences a social problem. For example, a student may not get along with his or her partner, or one student may become too dependent on another. In these cases, I spend a few days helping the children practice some negotiation and turn-taking skills. If they still don't get along, I change that pairing. While I want everyone to become friends to some degree, I do realize that some things can't be worked out between different personalities.

Children fall into many patterns before they ever come to school. Some gravitate toward quiet types, some toward loud kids, some prefer children who are similar to them, and others are captivated by those who are different. There are children who get along with everyone, and those who have only one close friend. It is not my intention to change a child's social disposition, but to give them the opportunities to experience many different personalities, no matter their own.

I have found that young boys and girls

Learning From Real Life

Too Much Help

Jasmine was a student with some serious learning and social needs. Elizabeth was a child who excelled at everything she did. She took Jasmine under her wing without any intervention on my part. Elizabeth helped Jasmine out, played with her, and included Jasmine in her other friendships. Towards November, however, I started to notice that Jasmine was taking fewer risks when she was with other students. I didn't want to break up Jasmine and Elizabeth's friendship, but I did want Jasmine to grow socially. I began limiting their time together by giving Jasmine some other partners. Elizabeth and Jasmine still did many things with each other, but Jasmine started to take risks again and bond with some other children, too.

Learning From Real Life

Friends for Certain Things

Barry had a best friend since pre-school. After first grade, his best friend moved away. When Barry started second grade he was miserable. His best friend had been very athletic, and they always did sports activities together. But Barry was very artistic, too. I paired him off with Dwayne, who was also artistic. They did a lot of drawing and writing projects together and developed a strong relationship. At first, Barry kept trying to get Dwayne to run around with him at recess, but it didn't work. Eventually, Barry began to spend time with a child from another class at recess and kept his friendship with Dwayne in class and on play-dates.

play together very easily. But once they get to first or second grade, a gender divide starts to occur. Best friends are usually the same gender at this time. It is not a universal truth, but it does happen more often than not. When children get to fourth grade, they start playing together again—until puberty hits—then forget about it! In keeping with my philosophy of flexible and varied group arrangements, I hope to help head off these kinds of issues.

I watch my children when it's time to choose a Thank-You-Very-Much partner. Naturally, they gravitate towards their best friends, or at least someone who is the same sex. I try to alleviate this with my opening remarks: "Pick a boy if you're a girl and a girl if you're a boy" or "Chose someone you haven't worked with in a while." We also talk about this openly during a few meetings. I have even had my students list the things that "only boys can do" and "only girls can do." We made a Venn Diagram, and every activity except going to the boys' or girls' bathroom ended up in the middle where the two circles overlap.

Nevertheless, when I partner children with someone of the opposite sex, they often grumble about it. Of course, as soon as they get started on the project, they forget about what their partner looks like and focus on what they are doing. Throughout the year, I try to use our meetings and groups as a way to reinforce the value of all children, no matter what their gender is.

Children with Challenging Behavior or Learning Needs

There are times when I worry about putting children with challenging behaviors in a group or partnership situation because I know the other students will have to help support and sustain them or will be distracted by them. While the benefits to the difficult child are clear, I have to weigh the extra burden placed on the more focused children. If I know that one of my students is rambunctious, aggressive, negative, or sensitive, I pay additional attention to where I place that child.

Every class also has some children with extra learning needs. My hope is to give these children the proper remediation in the area in which they are struggling. I try to do this in class utilizing both teacher and student support. If that isn't enough, I will also attempt to get them any supplementary assistance that my school can provide (such as resource room help).

As soon as I get to know all the students, I can consider the best grouping strategies for those with extra needs. I place these students in heterogeneous groups with children who may be able to help them, without compromising their own experiences. That is one of the benefits of mixed groupings. I also make sure to set up some partnerships in which an extra-needs student is the one with the more advanced academic skills. It's crucial that these students be able to share their positive abilities instead of only getting assistance. When a struggling

Learning My Lesson—
They Are Who They Are

In my first year of teaching, one of my students, Julia, was quiet, shy, and calm. Another student, Quincy, was full of energy. In truth, Quincy had no impulse control, was a bit combative, and didn't have very good work habits. I put Quincy at Julia's table because I thought she would be a good influence on him. There were also two other children at the table. Over the first few months of school, Quincy calmed down a little, but he still needed a lot of attention from me and from the children at his table. When I met with Julia's mom for parent-teacher conferences, the first thing I did was apologize for having Quincy sit at Julia's table. As I was about to explain my rationale for choosing this seating arrangement, Julia's mother stopped me. She told me that, although they were wealthy, she had put Julia in a public school because she wanted her to be exposed to all kinds of children. Julia's mother wanted Julia to learn about the differences that there are in the world, and to learn how to interact with all kinds of people. She also said that she noticed Julia had grown more compassionate and was coming out of her shell. Julia's mother reaffirmed my thinking, and also let me know that it was okay with her, too. I will never forget what she taught me. And I will never again apologize for children being who they are.

learner is able to exhibit certain strengths, it becomes an extremely positive experience. This may help build the confidence to try a more difficult task later on.

When my students are in homogeneously formed groups, a struggling learner can see that other children are on their level, even if it's only for one subject. Self-esteem is a huge problem for children with learning needs. They often feel like they are the only ones in a class who can't do something. When they are involved in a group or partnership with students who have similar needs and abilities, they start to feel more a part of the whole class.

One of the things that I do periodically is have the whole class take turns telling something that they are good at and something that they are working on. This gives everyone a chance to see that we all have strengths and that we all have things to practice.

The children say things like: *I'm great at building things, I want to try harder at social studies; I'm really good at drawing, I want to work on spelling; I'm a very caring friend, I want to stop calling out so much.*

I will sometimes write a list of what the children have said and hang it up in the room so that students can refer to the list and know who they might go to for assistance and who they each might be able to help.

GOOD AT...	WORK ON...
Artie:	I'm great at building things, I want to try harder at social studies.
Beni:	I'm really good at drawing, I want to work on spelling.
Ruthie:	I like the way I read like talking, I have to get better at subtracting.
Helen:	I'm a very caring friend, I want to stop calling out so much.
Harry:	I can write nice stories, I wish I could do measuring.
Karen:	I like figuring out math problems, I'd like to get better at art.
Alex:	I'm great on the computer, I want to practice sounding out words.

Being explicit about strengths and needs helps all children see we are alike.

Children with Special Needs

For six years of my career, I had the opportunity to work in an inclusion class. I was the full-time general education teacher, and there was a special education co-teacher. We instituted and developed many of the grouping strategies in this book during those years. Some students in those classes were classified as having attention deficit disorder, or as emotionally disturbed, learning disabled, and/or physically challenged. I've also taught children with a variety of needs in some of my general education classes. Students with special needs must have a chance to reach their potential and to become as independent as possible, while being educated in the least restrictive environment.

Grouping students in different ways greatly helps children with special needs. It gives them the opportunity to learn from others and to exhibit their own strengths, even if their range of abilities differs from the other children at their grade level. No matter what any student requires to help them reach their potential, allowing them to learn and play with their peers can only increase their chances for success.

The strategies for grouping children with special needs are not always different from other grouping situations. A teacher must take into account what the academic and social goals are for the individual students and for the groups. Clearly, there are times when a teacher must, however, make adjustments to grouping strategies in order to help these students to be more successful. Extra adult support to maneuver through assignments is one way to assist some students. Carefully placing children in groups with those who can help them becomes even more important when those children have specific needs. Switching some grouping arrangements more often, so that no children have to take on too much responsibility for others, is another way of providing good grouping situations.

Learning From Real Life

Community Building Works

Mara was a child who had some physical problems as well as educational needs. She limped, had very exaggerated movements, and didn't have a strong sense of personal space. By twenty minutes after the start of class, her clothes would be disheveled. Later, everyone knew what she ate for lunch because it would end up all over her. She was also sweet as pie and loved to laugh. Emmy was a very neat, organized girl. She wore dainty little dresses and always looked impeccable. From the first day of school, Emmy couldn't even look at Mara. My co-teacher and had been doing a lot of community-building activities with the whole class to get the students to accept each other. We hadn't made any concerted effort to get Emmy to be with Mara because Mara had some friends, and we just didn't think it was necessary.

Then, on a trip to see a screening at the planetarium in November, I just happened to be looking around as the kids were filtering in. As I glanced Emmy's way, I saw her motion to Mara to sit next to her. I was thrilled. Mara plopped down, put her arm around Emmy, nearly knocking her off of her seat, and the two were inseparable after that. In her own time, Emmy found the sweetness in Mara and realized she wanted her to be a friend. Needless to say, we put them at the same table spot and in the same learning center group immediately. This story still brings a tear to my eye and hope to my heart every time I think about it!

In my inclusion class, my co-teacher and I were always conscious of the modifications we needed to make and the support we needed to put in place for certain children. We also knew how important it was to make them full members of our class community.

English-Language Learners

There have been times when I've had students in my class who did not speak English as their first language. I've also taught students who knew only some English or were having their first experiences with English at school. The best way for children to learn a new language is to be exposed to it frequently. I read and talk to my classes a lot, but that is not enough for a child who is not a fluent speaker. When I pair English-language learners with other children, they pick up new words and phrases quickly. I make an effort to place these children in many different group arrangements so that they have opportunities to listen to and practice English all the time, and to learn as many new and varied vocabulary words as possible.

Cooperative learning groups are very beneficial for students who are learning English. The larger number of students and the project-based lessons require a lot of discussion and negotiation as children work together. This gives English-language learners many chances to listen to their peers and to get involved in conversations.

Formal partnerships can also be very helpful. Students who work together frequently get to know each other well. This can help an ESL student, because his or her partner will learn to understand them even if they are not fluent. The children learning English will also be more comfortable taking risks with someone they are friendly with.

I try to make sure that students who are learning English have a chance to read and listen to stories with the rest of the class. Students can often decode well above their comprehension

Learning From Real Life

Immersion into English

When it comes to non-English speakers, Ami was a special case. She had spent the first six years of her life moving around from country to country, living with different relatives until her mother got settled. When Ami joined my class, not only did she not speak English, but she had no primary language at all. She spoke a little French, a little Italian, and a little Mandarin. And without the basic understanding of how conversations worked, it was extremely hard for her to learn English. Initially, I had her spend much of her time with Jerry, but he got frustrated when he couldn't understand what Ami was saying. Then I tried Rani, who was very chatty. Rani just gabbed away when she was with Ami, who got very good at hand signals and pointing to things. But after a while, the girls started to have actual conversations. Because Ami spent so much time interacting with Rani, and Rani was so patient with her, Ami increased her grasp of the English language. Ami also spent a good deal of time with some other students in different group situations so she could practice, which gave her more confidence. Slowly but surely, Ami learned English and learned it well. She moved again after she was in my class, but she contacted me at school about a year ago. She's now living in upstate New York, attending high school, and taking acting and singing classes. Her English was perfect and so was her memory. She asked me if I knew how she could contact Rani. Anything is possible when you learn with other children!

level if their primary language was based on a symbol/alphabet system that is similar to English. I will often give these students a book in advance of our lesson, so that a friend or a student teacher can read it to them and discuss it with them first, giving them an opportunity to understand and participate in group or whole-class book talks.

As the teacher, I try to keep a special eye on English-language learners to make sure that other group members are letting them get involved in projects and conversations. It is easy for these students to withdraw, to observe what's going on without participating. I want English-language learners to be involved in all school activities and will practice good grouping strategies to help make this possible. I also speak to their families (myself or through an interpreter) to suggest setting up play-dates with English-speaking children or enrolling their children in an after-school program. There is no better way for these children to learn the language than by being with other children constantly.

CLOSING COMMENT

Being able to manage a class and grouping situations requires setting up rules and routines that make sense—and that will be handled consistently. By instituting procedures that are mutually agreed upon, you are setting up the parameters that will carry your students throughout the school year. When any ambiguous experiences or difficulties arise, you can then refer the students to prior discussions or assorted lists of regulations that may be hanging up in your classroom. These gentle reminders, along with specific rewards and penalties, help all of the children—and you—get through the days together.

As this book illustrates, working in groups and partnerships has many benefits for students. One of those benefits is giving the students the chance to see that we all grow and change, we all make mistakes, and sometimes modifications and adjustments are not only unavoidable but advantageous. I cannot stress enough the importance of remaining flexible in everything that you do with your class, so that you can make the changes necessary to keep your students' work flowing.

Making children with all sorts of backgrounds and needs integral members of the classroom community is one of the things that I hold most dear. All children deserve to be in an engaging classroom environment where they can be full participating members, no matter what specific issues or difficulties they have. Problems can and do arise—for all of us. Having to deal with many people in different situations is a natural part of life.

Future negotiators, leaders, communicators, and care-givers—learning now how to handle whatever comes up.

CHAPTER FIVE

BE A STAR

The Teacher Is a Model and Collaborator

I f you want your students to become "stars" as they learn about working in partnerships and groups, you need to model valuable partnership and group techniques. The teacher is the one who gets to shape the activities in a classroom, so you need to set a good example for how students should work together. In order for students to be able to work with many children, they need concentrated training with you and practice with other children. Using the kinds of exercises listed in this section, children can learn how to interact better and begin to transfer that knowledge to many experiences. As students develop the skills necessary for working with a partner, you can start implementing larger and larger group arrangements. It is essential to have many whole-group discussions, with you as a model, so students learn how to work with a partner and be productive members of a group.

Cooperation and collaboration are learned skills that need practice and negotiation. While students in a classroom become collaborators, they are not the only ones who get to work with others; as the teacher, you will need to combine forces with all of the other adults that come in contact with your classroom. Learning from and with other adults will increase the level of your students' success.

There are so many things that can be learned from other teachers and classroom aides. Family members, who know the children in a classroom better than anyone, can also provide many insights and ideas. There is tremendous power and potential in sharing information with a variety of adults. What better way to show students the value of working with others than by letting them know their teacher works in partnerships and groups as well! And be sure to talk about modeling; let those who enter your class know how you envision interactions in your class for everyone (not just students), and let families know—perhaps with letters home or in parent-teacher conferences—what you are modeling in the classroom.

Modeling Group Behaviors for Students

Getting Students Talking and Sharing

Most children love to communicate their ideas. The best way to begin conversations about working well with others is to ask open-ended questions: "What do you know about working with others?" "How do you think three children can do research together?" "How can you talk to each other about books?" "What will you do if there is a problem in a group?" It's important to teach students to express their ideas in different ways and to feel comfortable as they try out new grouping formats. When you first begin to discuss working in partnerships and groups, use yourself as an example in those conversations.

The students need an opportunity to discuss what happens in each of the varied arrangements so that they become aware of their roles in any group situation. All students, even the quiet ones, need to take turns practicing how to be group members. Since you will often be a member of a discussion or share, let the students know that you are taking risks as you share ideas, too. When students are comfortable and feel that their voices are being appreciated, they will talk and share easily. And when possible, try to make the dialogues exciting and fun; children are more likely to participate when they are interested and motivated.

Clearly, it would be a mistake just to tell the students to go and work with someone in a partnership or group without first giving them examples of the things they can do to make their experiences useful. Practicing techniques first, then going off into group work, gives students the chance to see what they can do in a variety of circumstances and situations that revolve around partners and groups.

Exemplary Activities to Help Students Learn How to Work in Groups

As I described earlier, I use mini-lessons or activity discussions at the start of most academic tasks. These are 10- to 15-minute whole-class conversations or training periods that teach a new skill or kick off a work activity. Below are the major ways that I help my students become familiar with group work. These can be adapted for your own classroom. And, of course, as you gain more experience in planning and setting up groups, I'm sure you'll come up with some activities of your own.

The Fishbowl

The "fishbowl" is the primary method for teaching the children in my class how to work in a group. I have some students sit around the edges of our rug and face the middle, "looking into the fishbowl." Other students sit in the middle of the rug, "in the fishbowl." Early in the school year, we use the fishbowl to practice how to sit (facing each other, shoulder to shoulder, in a circle or semi-circle) for different size groups. We rehearse the tone and level of voice that is needed for the particular activity, too. These first fishbowl lessons lay the groundwork for all of the grouping situations my students will be in for the rest of the year.

To begin the instruction, I become one of the members in the fishbowl. I sit in the middle of the rug with one other student to model the kinds of things partners need to ask, say, or do with each other. The forum for our first mini-lesson about groups is usually a book talk. Facing my partner, I open up a discussion about a book the class has just listened to. My role in the fishbowl is to help the students grasp the procedures for having conversations that make sense, remain on the topic, and are respectful of the participants. Throughout the year, as I implement new group formats, I put myself in the fishbowl so that my students can start to understand what I expect from them when they are involved in the new grouping situation. The introductory modeling that I do makes my expectations more explicit.

Since my goal is to have the students become independent of me for grouping activities, they take over all fishbowl positions in subsequent mini-lessons. One pair or a group of children then sits in the middle and rehearses having a discussion or working together on a project. At this point, I will merely moderate the discussion by explaining to the students what they should speak about, or by prompting them with questions and suggestions. The students who are "in the fishbowl" take turns talking while the children "looking in" pay attention to what they are doing. The observers sometimes help with questions and suggestions. Once the students in the middle have finished their rehearsal, we reconvene as a whole group, and I consistently ask the class these two questions: "What went well for the children in the fishbowl?" and "What suggestions do you have for group work of this kind?" By conferring about the specific positive and negative aspects of the fishbowl example they have observed, my students learn more about how they should act in a similar situation. Finally, after these activity discussions, the whole class breaks out into the grouping situation that was just modeled.

Try, Then Tell

Once students have the basics of good group and partner skills, we can start using the "Try, Then Tell" approach. I explain the activity the students are to do with their partners or groups, and then they go off and do it. We come back together afterwards, and the group recount their experience, detailing the things that went well and the things that were difficult. This is a more specific way to have all of the students practice a task, then brainstorm about the successes and challenges of that task. In doing so, the students have the opportunity to improve the routines that are needed for that grouping situation.

The teacher's role in Try, Then Tell is to supervise the discussions that take place once the whole class is back together. I ask each group to think about what they could do to make their work better the next time they work in such a group. For example, if the students worked on a math investigation, I ask each group or partnership to tell the class about what they did to investigate the problem, what part each of them played in the process, how they helped each other, and how they finished their work. By putting the evaluation process in their hands, I am helping the students discover ways to modify their own actions for future group work of this type, instead of waiting for me to help out.

Class Discussions

We have many class discussions about the different ways to work with a partner or group. During these talks, we all sit around the perimeter of the rug, and I will ask leading questions. I let the children respond with the ideas and thoughts they have about the kind of group work we are practicing. For example, when I teach the children to become writing buddies, I ask them things like: "What would you say if you liked your buddy's story?" "What could you ask if you didn't understand a sentence?" "How would you help your buddy edit his spelling without doing it for him?" "What would you talk to your buddy about to help her think through her topic?"

Group work helps students learn to communicate effectively with their peers.

Class discussions are also a great forum for creating lists for group work. I ask the children a main-idea or umbrella question, such as "What can you discuss during a writing buddy conference?" As the students tell me their ideas, I write them down. Later I copy the lists onto chart paper and hang them in the classroom, or type them up and print them out, so that the children can refer to them. Having specific examples like this available gives the students a chance to be autonomous during future grouping activities.

Role Play

While my class is becoming familiar with the variety of partnerships and small and large groups, I often have them role play what they would do in given circumstances. This helps students figure out ways to negotiate difficult situations when a teacher is not available. Role playing also illustrates for students the positive behaviors that are expected of them so that their partnership or group can flourish.

For role play, the bulk of the class sits in one area and the players "take the stage" like actors performing for an audience. The "audience" gets to watch the role

WHAT DOES A GOOD PIECE OF WRITING HAVE?
Check these out with your buddy.

| A PLAN |
| THE WRITER'S IDEAS |
| BEST EFFORT AND WORK |
| A NICE COVER |
| THE AUTHOR'S NAME |
| ALL OF THE DETAILS |
| BEAUTIFUL LANGUAGE |
| INTERESTING WRITING |
| BEGINNING / MIDDLE / ENDING |
| IT MAKES SENSE |
| THE AUDIENCE WILL APPRECIATE IT |
| GOOD SPELLING |
| PROPER PUNCTUATION |
| NEAT HANDWRITING |

Do you both have these things?

players act out their group experience, and then we congregate to talk about the things that went smoothly and the things that could have been improved. I find that this is a very effective exercise for children who need to become more comfortable with working in groups, or when there have been some consistent problems.

I sometimes become one of the members of a role-play situation so that I can help shape the conversations that I want students to have. When I am a part of one of these models, I often exaggerate my portrayal so the students can clearly see what they should or shouldn't do. (They love when I do that; it's fun and refreshing for children to see that sometimes a grown-up can be silly, too.) I ask the children to comment on my actions. They give good suggestions and never fail to correct my mistakes. Students often know what exemplary behavior is, but when they are working in partnerships or groups they don't always follow through. The purpose of role playing is to help the students articulate what they know about good work habits so that they can put it into practice later.

> **WHAT WOULD YOU DO IF...**
> ✆ Your partner wasn't paying attention?
> ✆ Your partner didn't want to participate?
> ✆ Your partner didn't understand what to do?
> ✆ One of the group members was taking over?
> ✆ One of the group members was really quiet?
> ✆ One of the group members was absent last time?
> ✆ Your partner or group didn't let you get involved?
> ✆ Your partner or group was doing the wrong activity?
> ✆ Your partner or group was noisy and unfocused?

Make a Plan

"Make A Plan" is a great way for students to think about what they will be doing before they get started on a new assignment. We talk about how to make a plan during class discussions, and then I ask the children to meet with their partners to plan how they will carry out the upcoming assignment. Partners are required to detail their ideas and work habits verbally or in written form. Throughout the year, I remind students to make a plan before starting an activity, and to refer back to their plan so that their work can continue smoothly.

> Our Plan
>
> Melissa- get materals
> draw out lines
> Shira- write lables
> do Colors

Put-Ups

Rather than merely focusing on shortcomings, it is important for teachers and students to look at what the class is doing well, and then build on that. It's easy to look at what someone can't do, but good group work also comes from respect and trust. If students only get negative feedback, they will be more likely to shut down. Showing my class how to use "Put-Ups" instead is a way to focus their attention on what their peers *can* do. During a class discussion, I model what a Put Up is. I compliment four or five students on something that they recently did in class, then ask the students to take a turn giving a compliment to another child. I'll ask them to describe how it feels to get a Put Up, and ask if they know what a put down is. Then we discuss the difference between those two kinds of comments. A good deal of our discussion is devoted to how it feels to get Put Ups versus put downs. By making feelings clear, the students begin to realize that they can and should interact with each other in appropriate ways.

After establishing that Put Ups basically praise someone's ideas or work, we also cite examples of what a Put Up might sound like: "I like the way you drew that house." "You are really good at multiplication." "I can tell that you know a lot about spiders because I really understand what you wrote on this page."

When the class does a share after a group project, I will often ask the children if anyone received a Put Up and what that Put Up was. This reinforces the use of positive feedback and from the students themselves, even when we are not in a class meeting.

I-Messages

I encourage my students to use an "I-Message" in order to get their feelings across without making another child feel sad or worried. Children are put on the defensive when someone comes at them saying things such as, "<u>You</u> didn't help me," "<u>You</u> knocked my pencil off the

table," "<u>You're</u> so wrong," or "<u>You</u> hurt my feelings." With modeling, I try to get my students instead to say things like, "<u>I</u> need help. Do you have time for me?" and "<u>I</u> saw you bump my pencil. Did you realize it fell off the table?" or "<u>I</u> disagree with that because...," or "<u>I'm</u> unhappy because of what you said. Can we talk about it?" Guiding the students to change the direction of a discussion from an accusation to a request for help or information empowers them to have much more productive exchanges.

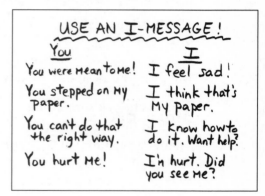

A Suggestion Is a Compliment

On one of my bulletin boards is a sign that says *A Suggestion Is A Compliment! It Means You Are Ready to Try Something New.* When someone makes a suggestion about what another person is doing, it can be viewed in two ways: either as a reminder of what was not done, or as a proposal about what could be done next. I want my students to realize that I am not the only one who can guide them toward new understandings and skills, so we practice giving advice to each other during mini-lessons. By verbally and visually reminding my students to talk about ways to help each other improve their skills, I'm helping them become a part of the teaching and learning forum.

Help—Don't Do

Another essential group work skill is to be able to share our expertise without taking over. We practice a "Help—Don't Do" strategy at different points during our meetings and classwork. The children learn how to work with someone by giving a student an idea, then watching that student try it out on his or her own. We model this process with a fishbowl mini-lesson. For example, let's say the class is working in pairs on science research, and one child in a group does not know how to take notes well. I would ask a student who takes good notes to work in a partnership with the other child. First, they would read a book section together, and the better note taker would ask the other child what she remembered, then help her formulate notes to write down. Next, the better note taker would take a turn reading a section of a book aloud, then write down the main ideas. Using the first two steps as a guide, the other child would then take a stab at reading and note-taking on her own. The partners would continue taking turns like this, so that each one of them has a chance to write notes while the first child gets used to the process. It is vital for the students to risk something new and then prove to their partner or group that they got the idea.

Group work encourages students to work with others and recognize individual strengths.

Group Work in Action

SOMETIMES STUDENTS MODEL THE BEST TEACHING METHODS

My students were making Guatemalan Worry Dolls for a unit in our ongoing study of "People Around The World." To construct the dolls, the children had to piece together toothpicks, then wrap strings around them. The class was working in groups. I was sitting with a group of three children, when I noticed Emile crying. I was about to walk over to Emile's table, when I overheard Tess talking to him.

Tess: *Emile, what's wrong?*

Emile: *I can't get these toothpicks to stay together. I don't want to make these dumb dolls.*

Tess: *I just got started. Let me do yours, too.*

Emile: *No way. I don't care if I make one, but if you do it, then you should keep it.*

Tess: *I don't need two of them.*

Emile: *Well, I don't need any!*

Tess: *Why don't we do it at the same time. Watch what I do, and then you try it.*

Emile: *NO!*

Tess started gluing together her pieces. Emile was watching between sniffles.

Tess: *Look Emile. Take the skinny toothpicks and glue them in the little holes on the side.*

Emile picked up his pieces and started gluing.

Tess: *That's great. Now glue two feet pieces on.*

Emile: *Okay.*

Tess: *Now all we have to do is wait for the glue to dry. Then we can start wrapping the string around the middle. Let's make ours look alike. What color should we use?*

Emile: *I like green. Can we use green?*

Tess: *Why not? How about you go get the string, and we can each cut our pieces?*

Emile: *Thanks for your help.*

TEACHER'S TAKE: While I was ready to jump in and see what was wrong, Tess was willing and able to get Emile involved in the project. Her initial offer of taking over didn't work, but her step-by-step instructions gave Emile the chance to do it on his own.

Accountable Talk and Accountable Work

In class, I expect the students to be talking about what they are working on, and to be involved only in the project at hand. We practice using "Accountable Talk and Accountable Work" as soon as school begins in September. My students learn that if we are discussing a math problem, then that is the only thing they should be talking about. If they are supposed to be writing a poem, I shouldn't see any Legos™ or clay in someone's hand. But staying on task is hard for young children; they have so many thoughts running through their minds. Still, they need to learn how to channel their impulses, and setting up an organized classroom with consistent routines helps students stay focused. Verbalizing and practicing what accountable talk and work means is a good way to increase a child's ability to remain on task.

During class discussion early in the year, I introduce the phrases "accountable talk" and "accountable work." The students and I brainstorm about what those terms mean. In the process, we discuss what it means to pay attention, to stay on task, to get into the activities at hand. After our first few talks about these ideas, I often stop the class mid-activity and say things like, "Raise a hand if you were just using accountable talk," or "Tell me if you are working on the project you are supposed to be working on." Occasionally, I will also say, "Stop, Look, and Listen," then call out the names of children who are working as they should. "I see Justin and Nancy writing quietly. I see Maritza reading a book. I heard Paula and Judy talking about the math problem." By checking in with the students during an assignment, I am reminding them that they need to be consistent during work times. When we gather together for various share times, I will ask the students how they can show the class that they were engaged in accountable talk and accountable work. Since I ask this question periodically, the students all know from the start that they may have to answer for their actions. We also talk about how accountability helps us all remain on task. Continuing discussions about the importance of accountable talk and work lets the children know how meaningful it is to stay with an assignment and motivates them to focus for longer periods of time.

It is necessary to vary the kinds of instruction used for teaching children about being with others, depending on the kind of grouping that will be instituted. It is also beneficial to review the level of success that students are experiencing when determining the types of mini-lessons to hold. As the year progresses, teachers should "scaffold" the learning about partnerships and groups to include larger and larger grouping formats. It also makes sense to go back occasionally and review mini-lessons to practice smaller group work that was done in the past. This reinforces and builds on what the students have learned.

The Teacher is a Collaborator, Too

*I*n order to establish the best classroom community possible, a teacher needs to utilize all of the people involved in that classroom—and in the school. Many people besides the teacher are a part of a class and a school. Those people have their own ideas, knowledge, and expertise that can help support the academic and social or emotional needs of the students. Other teachers, student teachers, support staff, and family members can all contribute to the good work that goes on in a class.

Since I keep stressing how important working in partnerships and groups is for students' success, it would be negligent of me to discount the role that other adults play in helping me succeed as a teacher. Collaborating with others gives me a chance to learn new things about my students and about myself.

Fellow Teachers

I have been very fortunate to work with some wonderful teachers over the years. I spent half of my career working in an Inclusion Program that combined 25 regular education children with 10 special education children. Together with another head teacher and one paraprofessional, I worked with the children in one classroom. And having so many children with special needs really helped me improve my grouping techniques. A lot of what we did for different subject areas had to be modified so that all of the children could participate in group work, and so that all of them could reach their

Fellow teachers can be a powerful resource—and terrific partners.

potential. Having another head teacher in the room provided more opportunities to support the children individually as they learned how to work with each other. It was also a wonderful experience because I was able to bounce ideas off another professional who was working with the same students, which let us stretch our pedagogical skills.

When I work with a teacher from another class, we meet on our lunch break, during preparation periods, or before or after school to plan what we would have our students do. The best way to get the two classes interacting is to set up partnerships that have one or two children from each class in them. Often the student pairs will really get into the task at hand because they enjoy having someone new to learn with.

During my last few years of teaching, the teachers on my grade have had regularly scheduled meetings. For part of the school year, we would pick a subject to focus on and then spend our meeting time each week looking at children's' work, talking about what we do in our own classrooms, and sharing strategies for ways to improve our practice. Grade meetings are a great way to get new ideas when problems arise, and to find out alternative ways to approach a subject. While my grade meetings were instituted by the administration, they might very well have been initiated by teachers because of their usefulness to teaching and learning.

Student Teachers

I am lucky enough to get student teachers from New York University or City College during most semesters. I instruct student teachers in ways of teaching different subjects and different kinds of groups. It is invaluable to have these assistants in the class for a few months a year because they can help one set of children negotiate their way through a group experience while I am busy with another group. Student teachers also give the children in the class another adult to bond with and to learn from.

Many student teachers I have worked with have also contributed to the class by proposing new ideas. The conversations that I have with student teachers help me to refine my ideas. I need to be explicit about things relating to different subjects and individual students and must think carefully about groupings, so it is extremely helpful to have another pair of eyes and ears in the room. Someone who knows the children well can notice the accomplishments and problems that some pairings may be having.

How Students Contribute

Each year, I tell my classes on the first day of school that *we are all teachers* in this room, and I will need their help to make this the best year possible. I let them know that I value their opinions and will always take their proposals into consideration. I commend the children when they try to work out a group problem on their own using some of the strategies that we have modeled, and I appreciate and remark on the times they come to me so that I can intervene in a positive way.

The students never cease to amaze me! They come up with all sorts of ideas about how to make our partnerships and groups work better. The students will suggest things like: "Why doesn't each group have one person in charge of the supplies?" or "My partner did the writing, and I did the reading. That really helped us." I always make sure to let everyone else know when someone comes up with a good idea. Children experience a variety of task challenges or social problems during group work. I want them to have the tools to negotiate these problems without adult intervention first. And when a child informs me that he has helped someone or that another student has helped him, I make sure that they tell about their experience during a

> ### IF YOU'RE HAVING A PROBLEM WITH SOMEONE, TRY THESE THINGS:
> - Ignore the behavior
> - Ask them to please stop
> - Move away
> - Discuss it politely
> - Ask a teacher for help

class meeting. This way they can model good partnership and group work habits.

As a class, we frequently discuss the kinds of things we can do to work out a problem. The children have some specific ideas about what they should do if a problem arises, and they often make signs and posters to detail the kinds of things that we discuss for group work. The four words I always refer to with my class are WHY, PLAN, PROVE, and TRY. Many variations of those words are hanging around the room because the children realize how important they are to everything that we do; see samples below.

Parent and Family Participation

In my first letter to the families, when the school year begins, I briefly mention the fact that students will be doing many activities in different groups. I send home weekly updates throughout the rest of the school year, often describing group projects that we do.

Towards the middle of September, we have a "Meet the Teacher Night." All the parents come at the same time, and I have a general meeting with them to talk about our class plans and goals for the year. I have the families sit around the perimeter of the rug, just as the children do. It is at this time that I ask the parents to volunteer to work in the classroom if their schedules allow it. The learning centers and literature groups are greatly enhanced by having additional adult assistance. If parents cannot come to class on a regular basis, I ask them to let me know if they would be interested in doing things at home (such as cutting out project materials). I also suggest that when they have some free time, they might come in for a one-shot experience (to help with a cooking project, for example). If my students have a brother, sister, or cousin in the school, they are always invited to our publishing celebrations, brunches, and pot luck dinners. I think it is wonderful for students to see our class as a family that encompasses children, teachers, parents, and siblings. When all family members know what is going on and take some part in our class, everyone benefits.

Twice a year, in November and March, we have formal Parent-Teacher Conferences. During these meetings, I review my goals for the students, discuss progress and problems, and check in with the families to see what they can tell me about their children. Conferences are a great time for me to talk to families about the ways that their children are interacting in groups. I explain to the families how their child manages their work habits and behavior skills during partnership and group work. This lets the family members know the kinds of things their child is good at, as well as what he or she should improve on when working with other students. I like to inquire about sibling relationships, because this gives me a window into the way the child interacts with others outside school. I will also take this opportunity to make suggestions for play-dates and study projects that the child can do with another student from the class. Of course, if any of my students are having problems or exhibiting needs at other times during the school year, I set up informal conferences with their families then, too.

Many family members appreciate the fact that their children get to be with a lot of students in so many different situations. However, a few parents over the years have complained about a child with whom their son or daughter is working. Most just ask for my rationale behind the pairing and are content with my explanation, but a few have demanded that I make changes. I realized that if they are expressing their concerns to me in this way, they must be doing the same at home with their children. Now, when I meet with the parents as a group in September, I make sure to tell them that while I always have a reason for grouping children, I can sometimes make mistakes. I invite them to share their child's concerns with me so that I can try to work it out in class, giving their children ownership for the partner experience. If this is not productive, then I let the parents know that we can talk about making changes so that everyone is happy.

CLOSING COMMENT

While my overall expectations revolve around the independence and interdependence of the students in my classroom, the role that I play as head teacher remains significant. The situations that I set up for classwork and social experiences can only bear fruit if I've taken the time to teach the children how to work through those varied situations. I need to constantly remind myself and my students of the best ways to achieve group success. The modeling that I do during mini-lessons and in general helps show the children what they need to accomplish. I make sure to provide ample opportunities for the class to learn about and practice partner and group objectives so that students will eventually master the procedures and become autonomous.

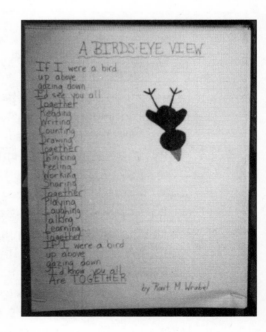

The collaborative process is the passage that we all need to go through to make our lessons and projects successful. I work with many people, my students included, to gain the ideas and insights that filter through to all of our activities. I cannot and would not require my students to learn and practice working in groups if I were not also doing the same thing. All of the interactions that I have with other adults involved in our class help me to be the best teacher that I can be and, therefore, help my students have the best year that they can have.

We all take turns revealing our strengths and ideas in all that we do, whether we are sharing during a meeting or working together on various assignments. Just as the sky is filled with stars lighting up the night, our classroom is filled with stars lighting up our days.

CHAPTER SIX

KEEPING (ON) TRACK

How Do You Know That Students Are Actively Engaged, Learning, and Sharing?

eaching and learning—of any kind—require a certain amount of accountability. As a teacher, I am responsible for making sure that my lessons are planned well, that my classroom and materials are arranged appropriately, and that my students are on task and investigating or practicing concepts and skills. As learners, my students are responsible for making sure that they are doing their best work, that they remain focused, and that they are helping each other out when possible.

Grouping children in so many different ways in all the different subject areas creates an extra obligation for assessment on my part. When all students work independently, a teacher can simply look at their individual efforts to gauge their dedication and progress. I need, however, to be diligent about my discoveries and evaluations of group work so that I know every student is learning and participating in the activities. I use a variety of strategies and tools to do just that.

Informal Assessments

Observation

My observation of what is taking place in the classroom at any given time is my primary means of ascertaining the success of my students' work habits. Although I must sometimes do some initial renegotiating of partners, what I see as the children get up from a meeting to do an assignment is my first clue as to how things will progress. I watch for reactions as I send the children off to work in permanent or temporary groupings for a discussion, a lesson, or a project.

As I observe students, I look to see if they seem happy or if some are grumbling, avoiding their partners, or refusing to join in the work. Watching these early responses gives me a heads up on how the groupings are about to work out. If I notice unhappy or resistant students, I quickly intervene, either by talking to the children or by making a change. My ultimate goal is to have students working together successfully and happily, so I use these first observations to determine if I need to step in.

Once the children enter into their project, I begin to move around the room, checking to make sure that each group knows what to do, and that they are getting involved in the assignment. I can generally tell who is having an easy or hard time working together, and I mediate any problems that I see. I may notice a student straying from a partner, ignoring the work, or starting an argument. Any of these signs would alert me to the fact that the student in question needs assistance. I will give the partners or groups a minute or so to try to work out the problem, but if they don't, I join the group and try to help get things back on track. Some students may need some confidence-boosting, skill suggestions, or support in managing work with someone else. Just by observing, I can decide what I need to do next to have all students on task.

It is important for me to know that the children are engaged in their work and are listening to each other. I determine these things by watching for appropriate conversations during partner shares and book talks. I make a point to notice if children are talking to each other during editing or study groups. When I see a group that isn't talking much or a child who doesn't seem to be focused, I get closer so I can better understand what is happening. These discoveries give me more clues about what my role should be next: Does the situation require my help and intervention? If I must intercede, I try to do so in an unobtrusive way. I'll approach a group or partnership that seems unfocused and just check in by asking how everything is going. Opening up a conversation without laying blame on any of the students gives the children a chance to refocus or ask for help.

During conferences with groups, partnerships, or individuals, I keep track of how the students I'm working with are performing. Later in this chapter, I will detail the sorts of notes I take and how I assess individuals and groups. These tools help me follow the work habits and patterns of specific children.

Observation is a powerful teaching tool. During my visual and audible survey of the room, I can tell if appropriate group work is occurring; then I can react accordingly.

Teacher Conferences

Conferring is essential to personalized teaching. It is the way for me to assess comprehension, to ask how students are doing, to help them plan strategies and assist them in their work, to support the interplay among group members, and to reconcile any difficulties. All of the skills, strategies, and activities that I present during whole-class meetings and mini-lessons are tried out in some variation of large or small groups. Therefore, I must talk to the students as they are working in groups so that I can help them put the things we've discussed into practice.

And while watching what the students in my room are doing is essential to measuring their interactions, the best way to specifically determine what is going on is by having a conference with a child or group of children. Discussion and communication are crucial in all endeavors—theirs, mine, and ours.

I sit and talk with children during all class routines and lessons. I try to rotate through the students over a certain period of time, depending on the subject and activity. My dialogue with students begins with open-ended questions that enable me to assess their understanding and give them some freedom regarding the direction in which they will take a project. I also use conferences to figure out if the children are applying the new skill or strategy that we discussed in our mini-lesson. I ask the students a few questions about their role and responsibilities in their partnership or group. When I close out a conference, I always make sure to convey what the students need to do or try once they are on their own again.

I speak with each student many times in a given school day. I once read somewhere that an elementary school teacher has hundreds of interactions every single day. Sometimes a few words, some encouragement, or even a quick suggestion are enough to get kids going and to keep them productive. However, a good classroom conference with a child or group, especially for literacy or math, lasts between five and ten minutes. It is absolutely essential to teach children strategies that they can transfer to other experiences, not just to give them a hurried idea for whatever they are doing at that moment. Conferences afford an opportunity to evaluate whether students grasp the concepts in a way that will be meaningful for them. Of course, given the number of students in a classroom, and the hours in a school day, it may take a week or two to have a dedicated meeting with each student or group in all curriculum areas, but this should not be a discouragement. I firmly believe it is more important to have valuable conferences less often than to have a few quick words more often. Having devoted conferences with my students is one of my greatest pleasures as a teacher.

In your own classroom, there will be times when you are forced to suspend conferences to deal with behavior issues, unfocused students, or personal needs (for instance, a child who gets a bump or a cut). There will also be times when you'll want to give special

---

TEACHING CONFERENCES

DURING EVERY CONFERENCE:

RESEARCH:
- from far away - what are they doing
- observe - what do they know - what do I know about them
- what was our mini-lesson about - follow up
- ask - what are you (and your partner/group) working on?

DECIDE:
- have a reason for what I bring up to child(ren)
- ask - why are you doing this?
- ask - what are you trying to work on?
- decide - the one main thing that we need to discuss

TEACH:
- what I think they should work on or practice next
- ask open-ended questions – get the kids talking
- use prompts
- support activities with suggestions
- give examples from lessons or other students
- ask the students to try out what we've discussed

SAMPLE PROMPTS and QUESTIONS:
- What are you working on?
- How is everything going?
- Who is doing what for this project?
- I notice that you...Tell me about it.
- Show me how...
- Can you tell me how you do this?
- You (and your partner/group) might want to try...
- What is going well?
- What do you need help with?
- What will you try next?
- You (and your partner/group) are working nicely because...
- Remember when we practiced...?
- Watch this...
- Did you see when the other group...?
- Why did you (and your partner group)...?
- How can everyone get involved?

Questions and issues for informative and effective conferences

attention to students who are struggling, or to those in need of more challenges. Because these situations invariably arise, I use the first month of school to guide the students to be more independent and more responsible for themselves and each other. We also discuss how it feels when a conference is interrupted and brainstorm ways to try to avoid both interruptions and hurt feelings.

It's important for a teacher to keep track of which students have had conferences. I create a grid with each child's name on it and several columns after the names. I sometimes prepare a grid for each subject I hold conferences for; see sample at right.

I keep these grids on my desk or inside my loose-leaf binder and check off names after each conference. When I have a conference with a group, I put a check, letter, or number next to the names so that I know who worked with whom.

	Reading	Writing	Math	S.S. Research	Editors	Word Work		
ANNA	✓	A	4	E	9			
BENNY	✓	D	8	B		✓		
CAROL		D	6	F		✓		
CONOR	✓		12	E	4	✓		
DAVID	✓		9	B		✓		
DAYNA	✓	B	2	F	1	✓		
DORIE	✓	A	10	A	2			
DUNCAN	✓	A	4	C		✓		
DYLAN	✓	D	6	E	1	✓		
EZRA			6	E	4			
FRANK	✓	B	1	A	3	✓		
HALLIE		B	10	D	5			
JAHBARI	✓		13	B	6			
JAKOB	✓	A	1	A		✓		
JEN		D	11	D	2	✓		
JESSE	✓	A	13	C	6	✓		
JOHNNY		B	5	F				
JORDAN	✓		2	A		✓		
KEVIN	✓	A	7	D	6			
KINARI	✓	B	7	F		✓		
LAUREN	✓	D	3	C		✓		
LENA	✓		12	B	2	✓		
LUCAS	✓	B	3	D	4	✓		
MOLLY	✓	B	14	F		✓		
RYDER	✓		8	C	3	✓		
SAGE		D	14	E		✓		
SAMANTHA	✓	D	11	B	3	✓		
SHAIYA	✓	A	5	D	5	✓		

- ✓ Marks indicate individual conferences
- Letters indicate groups I've met with
- #'s indicate partners I've had conferences with
* Notes on these conferences are kept elsewhere

Keeping track of student conferences

Student Conferences

A fundamental outcome of having students work in groups and partnerships is that there is always someone around for them to get ideas or assistance from. Children learn a lot about conferring from the many mini-lessons and activity discussions they have as a whole group (see Chapter 5). Every student pairing sets up a natural conferring situation. Children are great speakers. In fact, all teachers know that it is sometimes hard to get them to stop talking!

Students will talk to each other almost every time they have the chance. Natural discussions are a wonderful part of the learning process. There are times, however, that I want students to have discussions with a specific outcome. I set up patterned conferring situations so that the children can bounce ideas around and learn from each other about the task at hand. And by modeling good conferences (as I wrote about in Chapter 5) and giving students tools to use, I help ensure that they can have productive discussions.

Book talks are a great way for children to talk with and learn from each other. As I described in Chapter 2, book talks provide partners and groups with a platform for clarifying and expanding their comprehension of the different concepts of print. The point of book talks is for the students to be able to delve deeper into their understanding of a book through conferring with each other.

I often join in on these conferences to help train the students so that they can eventually become more independent, and then again to evaluate if and to what degree students are working together to make these talks productive learning experiences. Fishbowl examples are used to model the different ways to talk about books, and mini-lessons before book talks help pinpoint the specific strategies that I want the children to develop as they are talking with each other. Obviously the children must develop the patterns of question and response discussions necessary to have a successful book talk.

When I was initiating a series of book talks with my class one year, we brainstormed a list of the kinds of questions students should ask each other. These questions were prominently displayed on my bulletin board so that each time a group worked together they could refer to it. The list became an anchor in our classroom for book talks. Whenever the students were working together and they ran out of things to talk about for their book, they would look at the list and continue their conference.

As I sit in on book talks or circulate around the room, I listen in to see if students are asking and responding to these and similar questions, in order to determine whether they fully understand the purpose of such talks and are benefiting from them.

Partner writing is another effective learning and assessment tool. One time, the class was getting ready to write, edit, and publish some family stories that they had written. In order to complete their pieces in a timely fashion, the students would need to get feedback on the things they had done so far. I didn't have the time to have a conference with each of the students. It also didn't seem appropriate for me to be the only one making suggestions and corrections. I decided the children should work with their writing partners so that each student would always have someone available to confer with, and so they could help each other with all of the parts of the revision and editing process.

SOME BOOK TALK QUESTIONS:

- Why did you choose this book?
- What do you think will happen next? Why?
- Did you like the part when…?
- Why do you think that happened?
- Why did the character do that?
- What would you do in that situation?
- What does this remind you of?
- Can you compare it to your life or another book?
- Can you explain this to me?
- What does this mean?
- What was the book about?
- Did you enjoy the book? Why or why not?
- Which characters did you like? Why?
- What part was your favorite? Show me where it is in the book.
- What do you mean? Can you explain that in a different way?

The first day the students began to talk to their partners about what they had written, I made sure to circulate around the room. I noticed that while they were reading their pieces to each other and even giving compliments, there was not a lot of revising or editing taking place. The students had already done this kind of revision and editing for their individual writing, but they had never done it by having conferences with a partner. I gathered the class on the rug and asked them to generate a list of things that a good piece of writing should have—an "accountable writing" list. The next day I put a copy of it in each child's writing folder. When they got back to discussing their writing pieces, the partners were able to use the accountable writing list during their writing conferences to make concrete suggestions about each other's stories. The level of revision and editing increased dramatically after the students had this tool to help them as they worked on their pieces.

I take the time to sit down with my students to listen and sometimes intervene during their conferences. I am then able to judge the effectiveness of their talks and their comprehension of the task at hand. My comments and suggestions help to push their own discussions further. The things I notice during their conferences that need to be worked on might become future whole-class mini-lessons. When I know that the students are interested in a project, when I know that they are working on an attainable goal, and when I know that they are working collaboratively with their peers, I am certain that the kinds of talks and conferences they have with each other will help them to excel.

Note Taking

To be certain that all of my students are learning, and to record the things I notice or find out during a conference, I have a few systems for taking notes. I also use notes to keep track of the ways that my students are working with their partners or groups. This helps me to plan future grouping situations, and to determine when group membership should be a teacher or a student decision. All of the ways that I confer with and take notes about my students help me to pay attention to their progress and their level of academic and social participation.

Each September, I set up a small loose-leaf binder (labeled "Our Learning Archive") and create a section for each child in my class. I put four pieces of paper after each child's name tab. I label the pages with their name and a header: *reading* on page one, *writing* on page two, *math* on page three, and *group work* on page four. The binder is used for the notes I take as I have conferences with students, or as I see pertinent things taking place in the room. By writing down what students can do, what they need help with, and/or what I want them to try next, my future teaching suggestions and planning ideas become clearer to me. I am able to keep track of how students are working with each other as well, so that I am better equipped to help partnerships and groups maintain and increase their performance.

I sometimes purchase small spiral pads and use one per child to keep track of my individual reading conferences. I keep these spiral

ANNA	w/ Hallie + Lauren
BENNY	
CAROL	needs practice - will do well with Sage and Lucas
CONOR	
DAVID	w/ Dayna, Lena, Ryder
DAYNA	worked well with Lena, Ryder, and David last time - TRY AGAIN
DORIE	strong speller - put her with Jen and Jordan
DUNCAN	
DYLAN	class spelling helper - rotate through groups
EZRA	
FRANK	
HALLIE	strong speller - put her with Anna and Lauren
JAHBARI	
JAKOB	try to start helper/friendship with Kevin
JEN	w/ Dorie + Jordan
JESSE	
JOHNNY	can be in a large group of good spellers
JORDAN	w/ Dorie + Jen
KEVIN	try to start helper/friendship with Jakob
KINARI	
LAUREN	needs a partner who can be a leader w/ Hallie + Anna
LENA	w/ Dayna, Ryder, David
LUCAS	w/ Carol + Sage
MOLLY	
RYDER	w/ Dayna, David, Lena
SAGE	w/ Carol + Lucas
SAMANTHA	class spelling helper - rotate through groups
SHAIYA	

Spelling Helpers

Master note-taking sheet to record daily interactions with students.

notebooks in a small basket so that I can grab more than one when students are in guided-reading or literature groups. These are great for me and the readers in my classroom because I can show them what I am writing about their development, and we can then share ideas with other children. (And since I always record in the pad the goal or task I send the students off with after a conference, they can later look in their own tablet as a reminder of what they should be working on.)

Another way that I take notes in my classroom is by creating a master sheet with each child's name on it. I put a copy of this paper and a pen on a clipboard, so that I can quickly jot down things during a conference, whole-class meeting, or at other times throughout the day (see sample on page 99). Being able to review a single sheet that has information on each of my students, or on my grouping suggestions and plans, is very valuable to me. I keep all of these sheets in a folder, so that I can have them readily available.

Evaluating Students' Work

Folders and Portfolios

I try to use a variety of organizers to help gather student work. This enables me to scan their class work over time. I put student work into double pocket folders, and then keep the folders in different baskets around the room. Collecting these work samples makes it easier to review individual progress and needs. As I look through things that my students have done, I can also make new grouping decisions. Sometimes I want to create groups with students who have similar needs, so I want to see their latest work to make comparisons. At other times, I want to have students help each other out, so I will look through their latest work to figure out who has made progress in a given area and can help someone whose skills are not as advanced.

During each school year, I have my class do a variety of worksheets that I create myself or that I carefully choose and copy from a variety of professional books. The children also write in journal books, in reading logs (where they write a comment after each book they read), and do many projects with other students. These are the kinds of work samples that get placed in their folders. I am able to appraise the work of my students and their groups by analyzing these pieces.

For each child, I create a separate folder for their work in writing, math, social studies, science, and art. Certain groups who are doing research, or long-term partnerships, get their own folders as well. When student work is stored by subject, I can easily assess and compare progress in each subject area, and I can also have pieces readily available to share with parents during conferences.

By collecting and reviewing the work that my students do independently or in groups, I can gauge their progress and the skills or concepts that they need to work on next. After using the pieces in all of the folders for teaching decisions and conferences, I send them home in June so that families can go through them together and see the growth and development of their child.

At three points during the school year, I gather these work samples from each of the major curriculum areas and compile them in a portfolio. I sometimes have the students help me pick their best work in a particular subject area for their portfolios. The portfolio is a booklet with clear plastic sleeves inside. I place the work samples in the sleeves and send it home with a listing of the things inside. The families get to review these portfolios with their children, and I use them as a discussion starter for my parent-teacher conferences.

The portfolio work samples that were used during the 2000-2001 school year show some of the different things that the children did (both alone and with partners) throughout the year. Some of the pieces are first drafts, without any intervention. Other pieces have been revised and edited with partners. All of the science and social studies work samples were done during learning centers, in heterogeneous groups. When parents come in for conferences, I talk to them about the ways that each of the work samples were done, and we discuss the success their children had while working with others.

2000-2001 PORTFOLIO WORK !

These work samples show some of the kinds of things that your child is doing. They also demonstrate the abilities, effort, and progress that your child is capable of. Please ask the students to explain the entries to you. Happy reading!

NOVEMBER ENTRIES:

Cover-	Self Portrait
Page 1-	School (word web)
Page 2-	Beautiful Language
Page 3-	Character Map
Page 4-	Sample Journal Entry (revised)
Page 5-	Friendship Writing (2nd draft)
Page 6-	Math Sample
Page 7-	Communication Ways
Page 8-	Science-Machine Invention
Back Insert-	Love Is...

MARCH ENTRIES:

PAGE 9-	'STUCK' ON READING
PAGE 10-	LETTERS ABOUT LUNCH/RECESS
PAGE 11-	A STORY CONTINUED
PAGE 12-	MADE UP CHARACTER STORIES
PAGE 13-	TODAY'S NUMBER
PAGE 14-	MATH-HOW MANY LEGS...
PAGE 15-	SCIENCE-ELECTRICITY
PAGE 16-	COMMUNICATION-PHOTOGRAPHY

JUNE ENTRIES:

PAGE 17-	BLOOMABILITY
PAGE 18-	MY LAST JOURNAL
PAGE 19-	POWERFUL POETRY
PAGE 20-	WORD WORK
PAGE 21-	COMMUNICATION CONTRAPTION
PAGE 22-	MATH SAMPLE
PAGE 23-	PARTNER POWER
PAGE 24-	MY YEAR IN THIS GRADE
BACK INSERT-	AUTHOR STYLE STORIES

Progress Reports and Report Cards

In order to represent more formally the education, progress, and goals for each of my students, I do an Evaluation/Report Card at three intervals as well. While I constantly survey my students during all sorts of activities, I carefully assess their proficiency in November, March, and June. I use the information I gather to write a summary letting their families know what I have seen and what I expect from their child. The report card consists of a series of categories with letters that represent whether a child: is **A**-always independent at task or strategy and at proper level; **U**-usually has task completion or strategy use in work; **S**-sometimes does task or utilizes strategy in work; or **N**-never utilizes task or strategy in work. As I complete report cards, I look over many of the child's work samples in the different folders that I keep. I also review my notes on partnerships and groups, contemplating the ways in which each student has grown individually and as a part of our many grouping situations.

I then write a full-page narrative about the specific things that I know the child can do alone and with others, including goals for what I want them to practice next. I tuck this progress report into the center of each report card when I send it home. During my conferences with parents, we look through each child's portfolio and go over each report card as well. While report cards and narrative progress reports are very time consuming, focusing and reflecting so intently on each child helps me better direct my work with them. It's also rewarding to note all of the gains they have made. Sharing this information with their families is a great way to continue the school-home connection and to solidify the way each family supports our efforts. Families can then reinforce all of the friendships and group working habits that are being instituted in class.

EVALUATION FOR AND ABOUT SUCCESS

STUDENT'S NAME _____

TEACHER'S NAME _____ RONIT M. WRUBEL (ROE)

PUBLIC SCHOOL 3   DISTRICT # 2   CLASS 209-2ND/3RD GRADE

SEPTEMBER 2000 -JUNE 2001

Dear Families,

The purpose of this report is to let you know about the progress that your child has been making this year. As you know, your input and your child's input have been utilized, along with my own, to assess and evaluate appropriate goals and standards for each individual child. Where your child began in terms of knowledge, learning style, and group dynamics are taken into consideration to see what the next logical step in their development is. No two children are exactly alike, nor are my expectations for them, but a range of age- and grade-appropriate goals are taken into consideration for this evaluation. A portfolio of your child's work, daily activity, and teacher observations, are used to formulate this report. Please feel free to make comments in the space provided on this form. I look forward to seeing you soon. Remember that the important thing is that your child should progress from where they are, one step at a time. Each evaluation for this year will be based on the appropriate goals and expectations for that time of the year.

Regards, Roe

CATEGORICAL NARRATIVE LEGEND

N/A--Not Applicable for your child at this time

N--Never utilizes task or strategy in work

S--Sometimes does task or utilizes strategy in work

U--Usually has task completion or strategy use in work

A--Always independent at task or strategy at proper level

PRINCIPAL'S SIGNATURE _____

LANGUAGE ARTS READING

Enjoys Reading			
Listens and responds to read aloud			
Reads fluently			
Chooses appropriate books			
Uses picture cues for story			
Has sight word vocabulary			
Attempts new words			
Uses a variety of decoding strategies			
Self-corrects words			
Reads for meaning			
Retells in sequence with detail			
Writes comments			
Shares views in discussions			
Evaluates books & makes associations			

WRITING

Enjoys Writing			
Sounds out words			
Writes familiar words			
Uses illustrations			
Has independent ideas			
Writes stories			
Clarity in writing			
Includes details independently			
Increases spelling skills			
Uses spaces and punctuation			
Edits form and content			
Revises form and content			
Applies creativity to writing			
Writes for different purposes			

ORAL AND AUDITORY LANGUAGE

Attends to & understands presentations			
Connects reading/writing and speaking			
Uses accountable talk			
Shares insights/thinks creatively			
Interacts during meetings			
Accounts information clearly			
Applies information to new situations			

MATH/PROBLEM SOLVING

Uses many ways to figure out problems			
Chooses strategy that fits problem			
Verbally explains thought process			
Basic # facts quickly (at grade level)			
Knows place value			
Double checks math work			
Able to record process of problem solving			
Works in groups for math			
Uses manipulatives appropriately			
Knows patterns and geometry at level			
Chart/Graph skills (read and make)			
Applies new knowledge to work			

CONTENT AREAS
SOCIAL STUDIES / SCIENCE

Observant of environment and its impact		
Participates in large/small group activities		
Recognizes similarities and differences		
Learns about and appreciates culture		
Learns about communities / near and far		
Actively seeks information		
Makes careful observations		
Uses scientific process		
Understands/interprets info		
Retains information		
Applies info to new and different situations		
Locates and researches information		
Records findings in many ways		

WORK HABITS

Independent work increases		
Uses work time productively		
Does accountable work		
Plans work / proves responses		
Applies new knowledge to work		
Uses art for expression / creativity		
Attends to and follows directions		
Shows initiative		
Participates in cooperative learning		
Works neatly		
Completes responsibilities and work		
Remains on task		
Smooth transitions in class and schoolwide		
Completes homework to potential		

PERSONAL AND SOCIAL DEVELOPMENT

Expresses needs appropriately		
Seeks adult assistance		
Waits her/his turn		
Shares materials		
Gets along with others		
Plays and works with a variety of kids		
Helps anyone in need		
Regards authority		
Wins and loses well		
Observes rules		
Makes own and appropriate choices		
Takes risks socially		
Takes risks academically		
Focuses on needed areas		
Enjoys school and learning		

PARENT COMMENTS

1ST REPORT   SIGN _____

PARENT COMMENTS

2ND REPORT   SIGN _____

PLEASE READ THIS, RETURN IT SIGNED AND WITH COMMENTS. KEEP IT IN JUNE.

RONIT M. WRUBEL   1992   Revised yearly (current-2000)

Some of the objectives in each of the report card section are specifically targeted to assess the ways students are functioning independently, with partners, in groups, and during whole-class activities. Since all of these formats are crucial to creating the kinds of holistic experiences I intend for my class, I feel it is important to include them in these tri-annual reports to parents.

These are some of the objectives listed in my report card, as well as what each of them helps me evaluate:

- **Shares views in discussions:** evaluates book talks and participation during whole-class meetings

- **Edits/revises form and content:** evaluates how each student works with partners and groups to edit and revise

- **Works in groups for math:** evaluates math partnerships, math investigators, and math learning center groups

- **Uses scientific process:** evaluates small-task and cooperative-learning group work

- **Participates in cooperative learning:** evaluates particular skills for working with others

- **Shares materials/Gets along with others/Plays and works with a variety of kids/Helps anyone in need:** evaluates all of the specific partner and group work social skills needed to navigate through formal and informal partnerships

- **Takes risks socially/academically:** evaluates how each student does when playing and working with others

Proficiency During Shares, Meetings, and Discussions

In order for me to ascertain the success of the things the children do in groups, I gather them together for whole-class discussions. This is my way of making sure that everyone has made progress and done what they were supposed to do. It is essential for me to gauge how well all of the students are faring in various partnership or group activities; talking together at meetings is one way to accomplish this. Giving children a forum for discussing their activities also allows them to practice verbalizing their own process, which then reinforces what they know and do by themselves and with others. It also gives me a chance to evaluate how well the students are learning to formulate their thoughts and ideas so that these can be presented and understood by others. Good communication skills are essential to all of us—students and teachers alike.

Another benefit of having the students come together to talk about what happened in their work is that they get to listen to each other. The children learn a lot from their partners, but they can also learn from others in the class. When the students speak about their deeds in front of everyone, it makes public all sorts of skills and strategies. The students can then try out things that went well for someone else the next time they are in a group situation. During future work times, I can check to see if students have tried out some of the good strategies that were suggested during whole-class discussions. I assess how well and to what degree students have taken in and used new ideas. I have even seen some children remind other group members to try out new things as they work on projects and in groups.

There are different ways for students to share their methods and procedures after group or partner work. Sometimes after an activity, three or four groups talk about what they did. It is not always possible, nor is it always necessary, to have everyone speak. When groups speak up at a meeting, I determine their accomplishments based on the project they have done and the things they present. On occasion, I will decide to have specific groups talk to the whole class based on what I uncover while I am sitting with them during the assignment. I may notice specific strategies that I want everyone to hear and talk about because these meet the goals of that assignment. I may have assessed good strategies during the work time and want everyone to be exposed to those strategies during our share time. And there are other times when I ask each pairing to relate their findings. On these occasions, we either meet long enough for everyone to take a turn, or we spread the process out over several days.

When the students speak about what they have done with their partners or groups, I can evaluate the levels of achievement that individuals and groups have made with respect to their work. I judge this by noticing who is speaking up from each team, and by listening to what they are saying about their work. If different group members take turns sharing their information and strategies with the class, then I know that everyone has taken part. However, if the same child or children are always talking about what has taken place, then I will need to sit with that group to see if everyone is participating. The judgments I make about the success of group work informs my planning and decision making for every future activity.

In order to facilitate share times, we also do something called "Group Reporters." Before some activities begin, I let the class know that one person from their group will be responsible for telling all of us about the groups' work. Establishing a group reporter position lets all students know that they must be diligent about gathering the information necessary for one of their team members to tell all of us about it later. It also gives the children the impetus to evaluate their own work and the work of their group.

In general, I suspect that the more verbal students take over this task, and the quieter students may let them. But it is important that all of the children get turns speaking in front of the class, so I sometimes choose who the reporter for the lesson will be. After a few group reporter experiences, children begin to clamor for the job. They become excited about doing it, so I know that they are more focused on doing good work and learning what they need to know so that they can tell us all about it.

The students in my class know that they will have to come together to talk about their independent and group work on a regular basis. Since this is a fact of our classroom life, students become more evaluative of their own work over time. They want to prove that they have done good work, so they begin to check on their own progress and make sure that what they will be presenting meets certain assignment or personal goals.

The students also realize that I am observing how they are all doing in various areas. They watch me take notes, make suggestions, and praise certain strategies. Since they know I am assessing their abilities, they try to push forward.

Performances and Demonstrations

I believe students should be required to demonstrate their knowledge in concrete ways. Discussions are a great forum for sharing information, but there are many other ways to display information. Students can write, draw, or create things that show what they have been working on. This can be done individually or as a group. I sometimes ask the children in groups to work together, but to do their own note taking or creating. More often, I ask them to show that they are working with a team effort.

Doing activities together allows the students to get more training in taking turns, more chances to use their own strengths, and more practice in the areas in which they are less comfortable. By allowing them to do group projects frequently, I get to assess the progress each child is making in terms of their own skills and in their teamwork abilities. Having the children perform and demonstrate what they have accomplished for our class, for other classes, or for families, lets them show what they know.

Over the years, I have had my class work in groups to make posters about books, math projects, writing ideas, places we've studied, things they've learned, food groups, the five senses, and so much more. Posters are also a good way to get a lot of students involved in an activity. (Students like working on big paper, so we sometimes make murals too.) When a group does a large project, I can assess how well the students understand what we are doing, and how well they work with others. Theses informal and student-determined groups can provide a lot of information about how well the students are working with each other, including how effectively they make choices about who to work with and how well they progress in making new friends. And of course, each assessment of a partnership or group informs all of my future grouping decisions.

When we were studying the solar system, I created groups of three children. Each group studied a planet and did a report about it. Each day that they did research, one child was designated as group recorder. The recorder had to write down the pertinent facts that the other children in the group were reading and talking about. By having the students take turns writing, they each got a chance to practice note taking. By reviewing their recording sheets from each day, I could estimate to what degree each child was comprehending the material and writing about it. Projects like this also let me see which groups are producing the most work and are consistently on task. After the reports were done, the groups made a diorama of the planet they studied. They collected materials and put together some fabulous and creative scenes that fit in with the things they knew about their planet's size, surface, moons, rings, and/or atmosphere. We displayed the reports and dioramas in the room—and made sure to show them off to anyone who stopped by.

Culminating Experiences: Making Our Work Public

At different intervals during the school year, my students and I want to show our families and the school community what we are doing. After certain long-term studies or short-term projects, the class does a variety of culminating experiences. We then put together a presentation. Our class presentations take on many different forms, including plays, songfests, puppet shows, science fairs, and art galleries. It is important for the students to take pride in their many accomplishments and to share what they have done with all of the people involved in our class community.

One year we had been very productive: the students had made poetry posters, written fairy tales, constructed dioramas about different areas of our neighborhood, and made graphs representing a class-by-class census. When I asked the students which project they wanted to present, they couldn't choose. So we decided to make a museum in which each child would have a station near any partners they worked with. We then scheduled a visit from each class in the school. Everyone walked around to the different stations and got to see all of the things we had recently done.

We also hold "publishing parties." These have included Poetry Readings, Family Accounts, Character Stories, Genre Studies, How-To Books, and Newspapers. The children get up one at a time to read the piece they have written. The families sit around our semi-circle to listen to the wonderful things their children are reading. While each of these projects is not always done with a partner, the editing process and the ceremony itself are heavily group-oriented.

We have rehearsals for a few days before any show or presentation. I want the students to feel comfortable about sharing their work, and to have a chance to practice what they will do and say. During our rehearsals, the children get to give each other compliments and suggestions, which ultimately improves their work. We make signs, invitations, charts, gifts (such as bookmarks or pins), and programs that fit the celebrations. We invite all of the families and/or classes in the school to our events. Sometimes, we even use the auditorium or library space in the school.

Many of our productions are followed by a little refreshment. Each family brings in something, and we all get to discuss the event as we celebrate and eat. We usually have a bagel brunch with muffins, juice, and fruit. Sometimes I ask the families to bring in food that fits with what we are doing or studying. There have even been a few times when the students have worked in groups to cook some dishes in keeping of our project theme. For example, when the class wrote stories for existing children's book characters, the foods we ate were those that the characters liked (bananas for Curious George, pancakes for Nate The Great, crackers for Mudge from Henry and Mudge, and lemon pudding for Julian from the Julian stories). When my class did research reports on different cultures, we ate food from those cultures. I also have at least one evening pot-luck supper in the school cafeteria, so that we can all just get together socially. Of course, I always bring several samples of the students' work for everyone to see. Eating is very communal, so I feel it's a great way to cap off our projects.

Other than the suppers, most class functions take place in the morning so that as many family members as possible can attend. It tends to be easier for parents and guardians to arrange their schedules so that they can get to work an hour or so later than it is to leave early once they have begun their work day. And the children sometimes get nervous, too, so the earlier we do something, the fresher and less anxious the students are. I make a big deal about these performances so that the children will know how proud I am of what they have accomplished—and because I want them to feel proud, too!

CLOSING COMMENT

All of the ways that I evaluate the work of my students, and all of the ways that they share their ventures with me and with their families, are essential to the partnership and grouping experience. The kids love to demonstrate their work and their knowledge. By making our work public, students not only solidify their experiences, they also get to shine!

CONCLUSION

A WORD FROM THE STUDENTS: On Being in Groups and Partnerships

This is a list my class generated last year about learning together.

WHY DO YOU LIKE BEING IN GROUPS
OR PARTNERSHIPS?

- We get to help each other
- We can work with our friends
- We're never alone
- We can whisper and talk
- We get to know each other better
- We learn easily and quickly
- We can cooperate with other people
- We get to move around more
- Sometimes we choose our groups
- It's fun to be a partner
- Stuff gets done nicely
- We can do projects
- We can teach each other
- Great minds think alike (a phrase that I use often)

I remember feeling elated after the students told me what to write on this list. I wrote the list out on chart paper and prominently displayed it in the classroom for the rest of that school year. I also asked the class what was hard sometimes, and we used that information to help us in future experiences. As we were composing our list, I realized that even as the kids were describing their thoughts and reactions to me, they were independently grasping all of the expectations of group work that I had intended for them. To me, there can be no greater testament to the benefits—instructional and social or emotional—of varied groupings.

NAME: Frank Shanley
PARTNER POWER
WHY DO YOU LIKE WORKING IN GROUPS OR PARTNERSHIPS?
I like working in groups because you get to have fun and not be lonly and to work with new people everyday. Well not everyday. I like working with partnerships because it is not too loud or not to croaded. Oh and it is fun to work with other kids, I call that Fun. You get to work with boys and girls.

Make a picture of working with friends:

A BIRDS-EYE VIEW

If I were a bird,
up above,
gazing down,
I'd see you all...
Together

Reading
Writing
Counting
Drawing...
Together

Thinking
Feeling
Working
Sharing...
Together

Playing
Laughing
Talking
Learning...
Together

If I were a bird,
up above,
gazing down,
I'd know you all...
Are Together

—Roe Wrubel

APPENDIX

This appendix includes forms I use to help groups work well together.

Partner Power

Why do you like working in groups or partnerships?

_____

_____

_____

_____

_____

_____

_____

_____

Make a picture of working with friends.

Read Together

Draw and write about what you and your partner discovered while you were reading.

_____

_____

_____

_____

_____

_____

_____

_____

Author Study

Write about the author you are studying. What do you know about the author? What would you like to learn? What books has she/he written? What is the author's style? Is there a main character or book series? Do they do their own illustrations?

_____

_____

_____

_____

_____

_____

_____

_____

_____

_____

_____

_____

_____

_____

_____

_____

_____

_____

_____

_____

Great Grouping Strategies Scholastic Professional Books